ID0944700

BACKWARDS

Also by Nanci Danison

BACKWARDS Workbook

BACKWARDS

Returning to Our Source for Answers

Nanci L. Danison

AP Lee & Co.
San Diego   Columbus

AP Lee & Co.
PO Box 340292
Columbus, OH 43234
"Evolving mankind, one book at a time."

Dust jacket design: Jay Cookingham, Holy Fire Publishing
Cover photo: Bernat Armangue / Associated Press. Words of comfort lining the interior membrane of the 35-foot glass tower of the Atocha Memorial, Madrid, Spain. Licensed for use by AP Images.

Quotations from *Conversations with God* by Neale Donald Walsch, copyright © 1995 by Neale Donald Walsch used by permission of G.P. Putnam's Sons, a division of Penguin Group (USA), Inc. Quotations from *You Just Don't Understand: Women and Men in Conversation* by Deborah Tannen, Ph.D., copyright © 1990 by Deborah Tannen, Ph.D. used by permission of HarperCollins Publishers. Quotations from *Blessing in Disguise: Another Side of the Near-Death Experience*, copyright © 2000 by Barbara R. Rommer, MD, and *Journey of Souls: Case Studies of Life Between Lives*, copyright © 2001 by Michael Newton, Ph.D., used by permission of Llewellyn Publications. Quotations from *Living as God: Healing the Separation*, copyright © 2005 by P. Raymond Stewart; *The Power of Now: A Guide to Spiritual Enlightenment*, copyright © 1999 by Eckhart Tolle; and *The Presence Process: A Healing Journey into Present Moment Awareness*, copyright © 2005 by Michael Brown, used by permission of Namaste Publishing. Quotations from *Future Memory*, copyright © 1999 by P.M.H. Atwater; and *Fast Lane to Heaven: A Life-After-Death Journey*, copyright © 2001, by Ned Dougherty, used with permission of Hampton Roads Publishing. Quotations from *The Secrets of the Light: Spiritual Strategies to Empower Your Life . . Here and in the Hereafter*, copyright © 2004 by Dannion and Kathryn Brinkley, used by permission of the authors.

The author of this book does not dispense psychological or spiritual advice or prescribe the use of any technique as a form of treatment for physical or medical problems without the advice of a physician, either directly or indirectly. The intent of the author is only to offer information of a general nature to help you in your quest for well being. In the event you use any of the information in this book for yourself, the author and the publisher shall have no responsibility for any loss or damage caused, or alleged to have been caused, directly or indirectly, by the information contained in this book.

Library of Congress Control Number: 2007902729

ISBN-13: 978-1-934482-00-1
ISBN-10: 1-934482-00-5

Printed in Canada by Friesens, Inc. on 100% recycled paper

Contents

Preface

You may scoff at the idea of a person experiencing what we call the afterlife and living to tell about it, labeling this account hallucinations, dreaming, or wish fulfillment. I understand completely. Yet when the beyond-death experience I relate in this book began, I was otherwise healthy, wide-awake, influenced by no medication except the local anesthetic that caused my death, and had no idea I was dying. Therefore I had no reason to mentally concoct scenarios about what dying would be like. In fact, I believe I was chosen to have this experience precisely *because* I was healthy and in the unique medical and historical situation to demonstrate that the soul is not the life force of the human body, as is commonly believed.

Temporary death proved to me that the higher level of consciousness we call the "soul" is a separate being or species from the human being it inhabits. And we are the soul part, *not* the human part. The importance of that revelation is that our societies and cultures have been constructed around only one of the two beings represented in these bodies, the human animal, the less evolved of the two beings. And that must change if we are to evolve ourselves as well as our human counterparts to the next higher level.

A 1982 Gallup Poll[1] estimated that fifteen percent of Americans have had a "near-death experience," a term coined by Raymond A. Moody, MD, in his groundbreaking book *Life After Life*.[2] More recently, Barbara R. Rommer, MD, in *Blessing in Disguise*,[3] states that current research studies suggest between 9% and 15% of Americans close to death have a near-death experience to some degree. Clearly, then, having a near-death experience is nothing new. Yet my experience was unique, for it lasted long enough for me to personally *transform into* one of the Beings of Light many of us have met after entering the Light, and, I partially rejoined/merged with the being we call God. More importantly, I have gratefully received the tremendous gift of being able to remember and put into words a great deal of what I experienced. Those memories include answers to such fundamental questions as, "Who is God? Who am I? Why am I here? What is death?" And more.

The scientist in me identifies with those who assert that experiences like mine cannot be real because they cannot (ethically) be reproduced in the laboratory and measured.[4] Medical researchers have devised methods of verifying some aspects of the near-death experience by proving that after clinical death a person saw items or events their physical eyes could not possibly have perceived from the deathbed.[5] Scientists have not, however, devised experiments to study what happens after the spirit leaves the

Earthly plane. And modern science is loath to accept anyone's *memory* as proof of an event, possibly because scientific research and police work have proven how unreliable eyewitness testimony can be. To them, and myself, I say this, while it is true that the *telling* of the afterlife experience comes through the human body with all its weaknesses, the event itself is witnessed and recorded by a being *freed* from the limitations of human sight, hearing, perception, and understanding. No scientific instrument or recording device has ever been created that measures or records data from sources outside the human experience, as eyewitness testimony to the afterlife does. Therefore, to my way of thinking, science should have no say in the matter.

Every out of body, afterlife, and near-death experience recorded has been filtered through that particular narrator's vocabulary, education level, knowledge base, perspectives, religious beliefs, and communication skills. Many such experiencers have published their very personal moving stories, most of which portray "crossing over" in the expected terms borrowed from religion. Unfortunately, society at large tends to brush these authors off as religious fanatics or New Age lunatics, thereby justifying ignoring their messages. So perhaps it should not surprise us that our Creator this time chose a highly unlikely messenger: a trained "mouthpiece"—a conservative, midwestern, big firm trial lawyer seamlessly wedded to the American success story dream. Unlike previous messengers, I observed my own death with the clinical detachment of a jurist. And this jury of one found no evidence to support the traditional religious model of "Heaven." Instead, the reality I experienced was much more intricate and fulfilling.

You may be thinking, "I'm not religious, so this book is not for me." Well, this book is not so much religious as spiritual and metaphysical. The experience I had seemed more like returning to a different but familiar culture than anything I had ever heard about going to heaven. In fact, dying awakened me to a radically different perspective on humankind and our spiritual nature than was instilled in me during twelve years of Catholic education and decades of religious services.

Initially, I cherished my beyond-death experience as spiritual, and, indeed, transformational, but kept it mostly to myself. Its power compelled me to make drastic changes in my own life, including leaving my big law firm in favor of hanging up my own shingle. Now, after twelve years of soul-searching and integrating the experience, time is pressuring me to fulfill a promise I made myself before returning to the body: to communicate to anyone who will listen what I learned of our true nature and why we are here, so that more of us may understand that each of us has the power inside to change our life and our future simply by awakening to the wonder of who we truly are.

What follows is the true account of knowledge I gained while in a state we call the "afterlife." In the tradition of trial advocacy, I have repeated each major concept three times. First, Part I explains my understanding of each important concept from Universal Knowledge. Second, ways to integrate each concept into a new way of living appear in Part II. Third, Part III describes how I personally experienced the "knowing" of the spiritual truths related here.

For me, these words are not beliefs, opinions, thoughts, assumptions, theories, or hypotheses. They reflect my honest attempts to accurately convey events in my life as I remember them. These are my truths in my words, lovingly shared with you in the hope that some small part will resonate deep within you as it has in me.

To my surprise, many of the religious and societal beliefs I held before this experience turned out to be the exact opposite of the truths I gleaned from the Source. They are backwards. Moreover, our journey through life from this point on will be metaphorically backwards—back to the Source that created us. Back to the fully awakened state of awareness we left when we decided to temporarily enter into human life. For these reasons, I begin this account with the words, "We Have It Backwards."

October 14, 2005

Acknowledgements

So many people have helped make it possible for me to publish this book, and fulfill the mission I undertook when I returned from life in the Light, that it would be impossible for me to thank each of them individually here. I pray each of you will know in your hearts that your love and support have kept me going and made leaving the Light bearable. Some of the many wonderful Beings of Light on Earth who have contributed to this book, in addition to those mentioned on the dust jacket, are: Sydney Long, my first editor; Jackie Fullerton, Jane Strathman, Christina Potter, Sandy Lee, Shawn Reeder, Jody Cleary, Ted Henry, Carolyn Weislogel, and Amy Rued, my peer reviewers; Connie Kellough, who believed in this book from the beginning; my publishing "family" at A.P. Lee & Co.; and Amy Collins, my book advisor. A special thanks is extended to the many authors, and their publishers, who have allowed me to weave their innovative thoughts and words into my text, and, for the validation their words have given my own experience.

BACKWARDS

Returning to Our Source for Answers

Part I – We Have It Backwards

✳ Life Is a Matter of Perspective

For centuries philosophers and religious writers have taught us we have higher and lower natures. The higher nature might be called the "soul" or "God within us." The lower nature is typically labeled "human ego" and made to sound like a disease. We have been indoctrinated to believe that all our good traits are part of that higher human nature. We actually call good behavior "human," as in "human kindness," and "showing his humanity." And, naturally, we blame all our bad deeds on our lower nature–that detested human ego.

I had always found trying to discern the parameters of my higher and lower natures to be very challenging even with my lawyer and investigator skills. Often I asked myself, "higher as compared to what? Lower as compared to whom?" And, "Isn't it all just part of being human?" More to the point, I always felt asking me to use human will power and self-control to overcome human nature is illogical. What being can overcome its innate nature? Aren't we missing something here? The answers to these and many other spiritual mysteries came to me in the most dramatic and startling way possible.

I died—unexpectedly, in good health, and all alone, surrounded by thousands of healthcare professionals outside my radiology suite door in one of the nation's premier cancer hospitals. No one knew I was dead, including me. From my perspective life continued. But my understanding of it forever changed.

Before living life beyond death I honestly believed I understood what life was all about. My actions reflected what I thought was important—accomplishment. I was a National Merit Finalist in high school, earned two college degrees with honors and a doctorate in jurisprudence (law degree); made partner in a prestigious 270-attorney midwestern law firm; married a good-looking, brilliant California lawyer; and worked very hard toward earning a national reputation as a health lawyer. My sense of self rose and fell with the content of my resume and paycheck. How blind I was. And how arrogant!

Dying taught me so much more about living than my former existence ever could. Nothing gives one a better perspective on life–nothing–not intelligence, insight, enlightenment or religion–nothing teaches more about human life than leaving it. Living beyond the existence we now share catapulted me into a level of consciousness I instinctively recognized as "Home." Death revealed itself as merely an awakening process that immersed me in a previously unremembered place of origin with beings and knowledge my religious and spiritual studies had barely hinted existed.

What we call the "afterlife" is more accurately understood as the reality of our all-encompassing lifetime as a nonphysical Being of Light or Energy—a reality so profoundly different from human existence that we literally lack both vocabulary and concepts to adequately describe it. Part of that higher reality is an ability to know deeply the truths of the universe.

While I had access to that knowledge base I sought answers to lifelong questions of who I am and why I am here. The information entered my mind as *memories* of the source and scope of all of existence. I *recalled* answers I had known for eons to all of the metaphysical and spiritual questions that had plagued me. Experiencing life after death firsthand, and accessing these universal truths, imprinted upon my mind what no amount of human learning could ever achieve–definitive answers to all my existential questions.

Through dying I *personally experienced* that scholarly writers have not taken their thinking far enough when they characterize us as having higher and lower natures. The simple reality I *lived* through was a division between two beings, human being body and Being of Light soul.

What we identify as one human being is in fact a composite of what humans would perceive to be *two separate beings*. Each being is independent, self-aware, and possessed of its own unique inherent character traits, emotions, and nature. One being is the flesh and blood human. The other is a being composed entirely of light and energy—a Light Being that inhabits the human body as its soul. There are two different characters or natures within one body because there are in fact two different types of beings residing there. Each has unique inborn traits blended and creatively expressed through one observable personality that we collectively call "human." But there are actually two personalities vying for expression. And each has real, valid, innate feelings and natures that we need to understand and honor.

Perhaps you find the idea of two beings within one body too fantastic. Repugnant even. I did too at first. If you feel uncomfortable with my terminology, then substitute more traditional terms and concepts. Think of it as body and soul. Or physical matter and spirit. It does not matter what words you use or how you mentally divide the part that dies from what lives on into eternity. What is vitally important is that you understand that *who you really are* is the eternal part, the everlasting soul or spirit, the level of consciousness capable of surviving death of the body. You are not the body part! And because you are that more glorious Light Being life form you are not limited to the abilities and nature of the human you inhabit. We all have extraordinary talents accessible at will through the power of our Light Being essence.

We are in fact beings capable of changing the entire universe by merely acknowledging and behaving in sync with our own true nature. The power is inside us to help each other, our planet, and ourselves if we would only open up to it. Our human forms do not have to disconnect us from these powers. We need only move the human personality and emotions out of the way to experience a more enlightened level of awareness—that of our true Light Being essence. This is done via change in perspective. We can raise our level of awareness by simply shifting our perspective from that of the human host to the Being of Light within. And once we have done that, we have access to our innate energetic powers, including the ability to consciously manifest reality, to self-heal, and to live and love without fear. This book explains how and why this works.

Many of the self-improvement plans popular today rely upon will power and self-control to overcome human nature and raise us to the level of our so-called higher selves. But it is dishonest to ask a human being to overcome its true nature. It cannot be done. Nor should it be asked of any being. We all know this. We feel it in our bones. That is why most self-improvement plans do not work for us. They dishonor our bodies' human nature by seeking to suppress it. And, if you truly believe that you are human, even a human with higher and lower natures, then a life plan that characterizes part of you as unacceptable feels abusive and wrong.

There is nothing wrong with human nature. We Light Beings choose humans as host bodies precisely because we want to experience human nature, not suppress or deny it. Yet we are not without resources in our quest to improve our lives here on Earth, and to evolve both body and soul. In fact, we have an outstanding selection of tools at our disposal conveniently imbedded right into our very nature as Beings of Light. We can learn to access those tools and use them to lovingly train, not control, the behavior of our combined body/soul beings and bring about a new era of peace, prosperity, and love that I call the Third Epoch.

The understanding of *who we really are* that I absorbed from Universal Knowledge convinces me that we also have other basic lifestyle concepts backwards. For example, we need not fear hell-fire and damnation for our innate nature is to return automatically to the love of our Creator. We are not helpless pawns shuffled whimsically by a vengeful God, but rather powerful spiritual beings weaving our own life tapestries through choice. We collectively need a better understanding of the nature of our Creator, the universe, and ourselves in order to evolve out of traditional backwards fear-based human concepts and behave more in line with our own *true* nature. We must change our perspective in order to understand ourselves as well as life itself. That understanding comes from within. From our Source. It is pure, simple, and full of unconditional love. And it is unique for each of us.

What follows are my unique truths, my understanding of the answers I was given to the most fundamental questions of our existence—the same questions we have traditionally looked to religion to answer. Maybe you will find some truth here as well. Our journey starts with the very creation of the universe. "In the beginning," there was God . . . .

2

What is God?

Who is God? During my afterlife experience the entity we call God was not given a name or other form of identification. I came to understand it as simply the source of the universe. So that is the term I will use here. Whenever I refer to "Source," you may freely substitute the name "God." I rarely use the name "God" for our Creator, however, because the word carries with it an immense wealth of historical meaning, much of which is inconsistent with my new understanding of the true nature of the entity we call God. A new name is more appropriate to describe a new way of understanding the Source that I was privileged to experience in an amazingly personal way.

So, rephrasing the question as "what is the Source?" the answers I recall from the afterlife are:

Source is the Prime Being. It is the source of all and of which all things are parts.

Source exists as more of an alive, intelligent, sentient energy field than as a person.

Source is a universal being. It does not have a separate existence from ours.

Source is creative by nature and is the Creator of our universe.

Source exists as love in its purest, most unselfish state, and unconditionally loves us regardless of what we do.

Source generates an aura we experience as sublime bliss—happiness beyond our wildest dreams.

Source by nature has unlimited curiosity and an unlimited quest for experience.

Prime Being. First of all, Source is the source of all life. All intelligence. All emotions. All self-awareness. All knowing. All experience. All energy. All matter. All everything. It is what we have always thought of as a Supreme Being. It is the source from whence all things come and of which all things are still part.

Collective Being. Source is universal by nature. During my beyond-death experience I came to understand that Source is not a discrete, separate-from-us God-person as religions characterize "him." Human religion has this concept totally backwards. I received "knowing" that God is actually more of an enormous entity than a singular, individual, discrete person. Source is more akin to what we could call an *intelligent, self-aware, emotional energy source,* or an *alive field of energy.* God is not a person in the way humans think of themselves as individual persons.

In fact, Source is not an individual at all. God/Source is simultaneously **both** a single, unified *field* of energy **and** a collective being composed of all of creation, including us. In other words, there is only **one** being in our universe.[6] All that exists in the universe, known and unknown to us, is part of the one being we have traditionally called God and I now call Source. All that exists constitutes One Being—Source.

The Source I experienced firsthand is pure living, feeling energy–pure Being of Light and Energy. And that Source exquisitely loves us, accepts us, and is in fact *constructed of us as a collective whole.* We are literally part of the Source! *We* are part of God! We make up part of its energy field/being in the same way the air inside your house is part of the atmosphere, or an inlet of seawater on the beach is part of the ocean. Source does not exist separate and apart from us. The following words of fellow beyond-death experiencer Richard L summarize beautifully the true nature of Source as I perceived it up close:

> We are all expressions of God. When you see with your eyes, you see through the eyes of God and he experiences reality through yours. When you speak to God, you speak to yourself. We are one and the same, there is no division or separation. You can no more "see" God than your hand can see you, for it is a part of you and functions because of you and for your purposes, as well as it's own. There is no separation. Any that seems to exist is an illusion.[7]

Creative Being. Source is the creator of the universe as we have come to know it—all that we see, hear, feel, taste, touch and experience as human life. Source also created all that we cannot perceive with a human's limited senses, including our very beings,

13

all the dimensions invisible to us, and all the energy of which we are aware and unaware. Source used "attention and intention" to create these things out of its own Energy through the process called "manifesting." Source manifested its will that each thing exist, and so it did. Source's thoughts and intentions manifested into reality all of creation.

How do thoughts create a universe? Manifesting reality is a skill unique to Beings of Light, including the Prime Light Being called Source. Source, and to a more limited extent all Light Beings, can focus attention and intention like a laser beam to concentrate thought energy into various physical forms for extended or limited periods of time.

The closest analogy between manifesting and a human experience may be dreaming, though use of that word automatically erroneously conveys the absence of reality, when manifesting does in fact create reality as humans understand it. So do not misunderstand my use of the dreaming concept here. Use dreaming only as a framework that lends general shape to the much larger and more complicated phenomenon of manifesting actual reality.

When you dream, your thoughts construct an entire universe of people, places, and things. You populate dreams with characters of your choice, usually including yourself. Dream events, especially nightmares, can seem very real at the time. You have genuine emotional responses during dreams. If you awake in the middle of one you might feel disoriented, and not know where you are for a moment, because it feels so real. You have, in effect, manifested a universe in your dream and it was your whole reality for as long as it lasted.

The Source's "dream," for lack of a better term, is our whole universe. And just as our dreams are an integral part of our thoughts, the universe is an integral part of Source's thoughts. Our universe is not actually a *dream* like the ones we experience as human beings. Dreaming is just an example with which we are all familiar that demonstrates how an environment and characters can be created out of pure thought and still seem very real to us.

At the beginning of what we call creation, Source focused its creative attention on thoughts of a universe, manifesting thought-forms of various vibrational levels or energy signatures in a manner somewhat similar to how we construct our dreams from thought-forms of environments and people. Source infused some of the vibrational levels with its own self-awareness, much like you might play one or more roles in your dreams. These different bits of Source thought did not actually *separate* from the Source any more than your own dreams separate from you. Dreams cannot exist without your mind creating them. Similarly, Source's thoughts and all the vibrational levels they create remain eternally connected to the Source.

In the words of author and spiritual teacher P. Raymond Stewart:

Every person and every form is but an idea in the mind of God. Each person originates from Spirit as consciousness. Consciousness begets thought. Thought takes form. Although we perceive our bodies to be separate from one another, we are all just different forms projected from the same universal consciousness. Because of this, we are not static, not inflexible person-boxes, but can change with a change of thought.[8]

Creation is closer in analogy to the stretching of an infinitely large rubber band than to the "big bang" theory of scientists in which matter dispersed in segregated fragments. Think of the sun and its beams of light. Sunbeams stream down from the sun to Earth in energy waves that are still connected to the sun. We feel the energy on our skin in the form of warmth. Warmth from the sun. Sunlight is a continuous stream of solar heat. Source thought-forms are still connected to Source in somewhat the same way. You could call them "Sourcebeams"—creative bits of Source "Energy" manifested to vibrate at varying frequencies so different thought-forms are able to exhibit somewhat individual characteristics. Your dreams work the same way, in that you form mental energy (thoughts) into pictures (forms) so they can interact as separate individuals in your dream drama.

With Sourcebeams, the slower their vibration oscillates the more solid they *appear* to human senses. There is no solid matter per se; it is only the limitations of human sensory organs that make some vibrations of Source Energy appear solid to us. As an analogy, think of it as the reverse phenomenon of flipping a stack of single frames of pictures very quickly to make the characters appear to move, which is how cartoons are made. Now reverse the process so that the pictures are flipping so slowly that the image appears to stand still. We call that perception solid matter, even though the pictures are still flipping too slowly for the human eye to see.

We have labeled some of the slowest Energy signatures humans perceive as planets, moons, and asteroids, and have lumped them together with all the other items we see every day, such as trees, cars, furniture, and clothes, under the heading "physical matter." Some of the faster vibrating physical matter we call suns, stars, nebula, and gas giants. Even faster Energy signatures cannot be seen with human eyes, and are identified only through scientific means. They include radio waves, microwaves, electromagnetic fields, atoms, and the tiny energy bonds that hold molecules together. A few alternative medicine professionals acknowledge the existence of even faster Energy vibrations, such as the chakras, auras, and energy fields surrounding the body. So far, however, only religion has recognized the highest or fastest vibrations—those we call God/Source and souls.

Source created our universe because it is simply its nature to create. The universe is creation born of pure joy and the thrill of witnessing one's own thoughts manifested into reality. Source's insatiable curiosity inspired it to spin and weave an energetic tapestry of immense intricacy and wonder. Source's purpose is to delight not only itself as a unified Being of Light, but also itself as a Collective Being composed of all the bits of self-awareness invested into thought-forms populating the universe like characters in a dream.

Human beings are one form of Energy signature manifested by Source to vibrate at a certain frequency. That frequency is different, and much slower, than the Source's vibrational frequency, which accounts for humans' appearance as solid matter. Other beings are manifested to vibrate at frequencies closer to that of the Source itself, i.e., the Beings of Light I met during my beyond death adventure. (See Chapter 21.) We already know one aspect of these Light Beings by another name—souls. Souls are the result of Light Beings choosing to lower part of their Energy to a level where it can invisibly combine with a human being. (See Chapter 3.)

All of the thought Energy Source spread out to form the universe, all the Sourcebeams, are intended to evolve and are evolving back to the Source in a kind of cosmic boomerang effect. It is the very nature of Source manifestations to follow a cycle of out and then back in again, like a rubber band stretching then contracting. We see this phenomenon every day in cycles of seasons; the birth to death cycle of animals, plants, and human beings; and the cycles of creation and destruction in the universe at large. Everything eventually returns to the Source's vibrational level and so follows a cycle extending out from it and returning back to it. It is the nature of energy to attract itself, to seek out its source. Think about the electricity in our homes. If the electrical circuit is complete, electricity makes a circle unto itself and hums along elegantly and efficiently. If we cut the cord, for example, we say we short circuit the flow, or there is a "short." Bringing the cut ends close together may cause the electricity to arc to complete the circuit and return to its continuous flow.

Sourcebeams likewise seek continuity with Source. The difference is that Sourcebeam Energy vibrates at different frequencies and so cannot arc back into continuity with Source until the frequencies harmonize. All Energy vibrations must eventually increase as they boomerang back toward merger into Source, which exists at the highest vibrational level. Consequently, all matter is eternally evolving and changing as it journeys back to reunification with Source, leaving former versions of itself behind. Scientists might describe one part of this cycle by saying certain Energy signatures are decaying, such as a radioisotope decays. But, as I understand it, each type of Energy's signature is not decaying, but rather changing in a way consistent with its evolutionary path. For example, a stellar nursery may "decay" into galaxies, which might then evolve into a field of stars and planets. This is the evolutionary path of deep space.

Planet Earth is evolving too. I personally observed that Earth epochs end when its vibrational evolution gets off track or mutates due to Energy imbalances. I saw that this was what caused the dinosaurs and first version of the human species to be wiped out at the end of the First Earth Epoch. A similar evolutionary imbalance is currently underway, which will result in the end of the Second Earth Epoch and beginning of the third as I saw in a review of Earth's history that I experienced during my beyond-death experience. (See Chapter 21.)

Human beings evolve through the "decay" or change in energy signature of DNA to produce different variations in the species. During my beyond-death experience I witnessed Earth as having supported two separate successful evolutions of humanity, with a third currently in progress. The evolutionary path for humans so far this epoch has been maximizing use of their brains, emotions, and physical dexterity. Ultimately, our own evolution will change humans into a more intellectual, emotionally mature, and less physical version of the species to be compatible with the Third Epoch. We inhabit the second version of humans, which in a way is an endangered species. But, we still have the power individually and collectively to consciously evolve our human hosts into harmony with our true Light nature and thereby increase the happiness and love in the current Second Earth epoch. Some of us may even evolve enough to participate in the Third Earth Epoch of peace and joy.

All of Source Energy, no matter its form or evolutionary path, will ultimately increase to the Source's vibrational level and merge back into Source. These literal reunions with the Source's own

Energy field is a fundamental concept unknown to me before my beyond-death experience, because I had believed in the human idea of a God who is a separate person from us. But I learned a different and more wonderful perspective. Source is not separate from its creations and never has been. Source continues to exist in and through its manifestations–regardless of how far or near they appear to wander.

Why have we mischaracterized Source for so long? Because most of the time we operate in what I call "human mode," meaning we allow human nature to predominate our thoughts and feelings. In human mode, we are limited in intellectual capacity by our host bodies. Our concepts are restricted to the building blocks of human experience and perception. So, we have created a concept of God that mirrors the human species in many ways. Whereas the Bible talks about God making man in his own image, humans have similarly "made" a concept of God in human image. P. Raymond Stewart eloquently describes in *Living as God* how deeply we have deceived ourselves about the nature of Source by restricting our thinking to human mode:

> You are God. This is the obvious truth we do not hear, clearly expressed and demonstrated by masters we have ignored. God being love extends Itself naturally to create All That Is. This is the great insight we prevent ourselves from having, going as far as creating institutions and religions to keep us from seeing it. Why? Because to accept this truth would mean the death of all we have been

conditioned to believe. It would mean the end of our current perception of who we have come to see ourselves as—separate, vulnerable, limited persons needing to struggle and defend ourselves against "others" to exist. There would be no more conflict, no more aggression, no more drama, no more unease, displeasure, or even disease if we were to accept our Oneness—our Oneness as God.[9]

Some people actually believe Source is male. Others attach racial features. Many of us think of God/Source behaving like a human parent towards his children. I find this concept of God so far from the truth as to be literally damaging to our spiritual health. The Source I experienced firsthand is neither male nor female. Nor is it neuter. Gender has no application to it any more than gender applies to the air we breathe. In fact, our attempts to attribute gender and other human characteristics to Source have, in my opinion, severely damaged our comprehension of our Creator and ourselves and thereby retarded our spiritual evolution.

While I understand that personification of a deity helps give the common man something to relate to, it backfires by reducing the Source of our existence to actions and motivations in common with the lowest and most unloving behaviors of humankind. For example, some depict Source as a loving father figure in an attempt to convey pictorially our relationship to "him." But that image pulls into itself both the positive and the negative connotations various individuals have of maleness and fatherhood. Casting God/Source into a male role also subliminally broadcasts male superiority, and has, in fact, been taken precisely that way by some religions. But Source has nothing in common with human males. Or with human females for that matter. Source is a completely energetic non-physical Being with no gender-specific traits.

Loving Being. The father figure concept of God also conveys a false impression of how Source loves us. Everyone has his/her own experience with fatherly love, or the lack thereof. Even the best parent fails a child on occasion. But Source's love never fails, is never withheld, and is always given on a far grander scale than we can imagine. Source love is complete, unrestricted, non-judging, unconditional, and fulfilling. Source personifies joyous, warm, immeasurable love. It is love like you cannot even imagine while in human mode. The greatest passion you ever experienced on Earth cannot compare. The power of a parent's love for his or her child pales in comparison to Source love. Such examples of human love are but a small taste on the tip of a tongue when compared to the richness of Source love.

The father figure image used for God similarly creates a false impression of Source because it implies a mundane parental supervisory role, when that could not be farther from the reality I experienced. Neale Donald Walsch's New York Times best-selling book *Conversations with God: An Uncommon Dialogue, Book 1* vividly recounts the origin of this misperception:

It was your parents who taught you that love is

conditional—you have felt their conditions many times—and that is the experience you take into your own love relationships.

It is also the experience you bring to Me.

From this experience you draw your conclusions about Me. Within this framework you speak your truth. "God is a loving God," you say, "but if you break His commandments, He will punish you with eternal banishment and everlasting damnation."

For have you not experienced the banishment of your own parents? Do you not know the pain of their damnation? How, then could you imagine it to be any different with Me?

You have forgotten what it was like to be loved without condition. You do not remember the experience of the love of God. And so you try to imagine what God's love must be like, based on what you see of love in the world.

You have projected the role of "parent" onto God, and have thus come up with a God Who judges and rewards or punishes, based on how good He feels about what you've been up to. But this is a simplistic view of God, based on your mythology. It has nothing to do with Who I Am.[10]

Throughout my beyond-death experience and close contact with Source I understood that God is not judging, or controlling, or in any way micromanaging our lives. We ascribe those *human* character traits to Source because our current experience is limited to observation of human behavior. We have "humanized" the God of our understanding precisely so that we can understand, and ultimately "control," our relationship with Source. Religions based on human experience have taught us that God expects us to conform to a prescribed set of rules. Thus, we believe we can control our destiny after death and enter Heaven by following those rules. That, in effect, is an attempt to control God's alleged judgment of us. We believe we will be granted access to Heaven if we do as we are told, based upon our human experience that we may stay up until 10:00 pm if we do our homework, or Dad will give us the car keys if we clean up our room. These human analogies demonstrate the type of conditional love we have all known since birth into our human hosts.

Such conditional parental love has no counterpart with Source. Source exercises no supervisory role over us, like a parent does, because it is not training us to fit into anything (like human society). We are already perfectly suited for Source "society" just by virtue of our nature. Similarly, Source has no reason to dictate our behavior like a father might. It does not tell us what to do, in a specified set of rules or otherwise. There is no need for such rules because *it is our very nature* to return to the Source regardless of what we do. **Regardless** of what we do. We do not have to earn our place with God. We already *are* part of it! That is Source's and our very nature.

Source love is far more than an emotion emanating from one being in response to another, which is how we view love while in human mode. Source love is a form of existence. A state of being. Perhaps it is what religion calls the "state of grace." When I entered the Light, Source love permeated my very molecules and increased my vibrational level to an ecstasy of joy and bliss. Our creator loves every miniscule morsel of its creations with intensity beyond the brilliance of the sun, beyond the depth of space, and beyond human imagination.

Blissful Being. Source is innately and perpetually happy. Blissful happiness. Source exudes waves of joy and serenity that permeate its energy field, part of which we call "the Light." That joy is both fulfilling and healing. Every near-death and afterlife experiencer who enters into the Light reports becoming intoxicated with happiness just to be in closer proximity to Source.

Curious Being. The Source I experienced is the most curious and inquisitive being/entity you could ever imagine. Part III describes what it was like for me to live in the Light and how wonderful it was. Yet I explain that I missed some aspects of the human condition. I missed the feel of skin, physical touching, eating, and temperature variations. In much the same way, Source wanted to know what it felt like to experience life at slower vibrations, such as that of human beings, and to have the illusion of being physical matter.

Source similarly longed to know what separateness felt like, an understandable goal for a being alone in a universe. Source created our universe simply to know itself from different, separate, perspectives. Curiosity inspired Source to subdivide itself into little bits of Sourcebeams that could be slowed down enough to experience a type of artificial separateness. (See Chapter 4 for more detail.)

Conversations with God, which I read many years after my beyond-death experience, echoes in what is to me warmly familiar terms how and why Source/God created our universe:

> This *energy*–this pure, unseen, unheard, unobserved, and therefore unknown-by-anyone-else energy–chose to experience Itself as the utter magnificence It was. In order to do this, It realized It would have to use a reference point *within*.
>
> It reasoned, quite correctly, that any *portion* of Itself would necessarily have to be *less than the whole*, and that if It thus simply *divided* Itself into portions, each portion, being less than the whole, could look back on the rest of Itself and see magnificence.
>
> And so All That Is divided Itself–becoming, in one glorious moment, that which is *this*, and that which is *that*. For the first time, *this* and *that* existed, quite apart from each other. And still, both existed simultaneously. . . .
>
> In rendering the universe as a *divided version of Itself*, God produced, from pure energy, all that now exists–both seen and unseen.
>
> In other words, not only was the physical universe thus created, *but the metaphysical universe as well*. The part of God which forms the second half of the Am/Not Am equation also exploded into an infinite number of units smaller than the whole. These energy units you would call spirits. . . .
>
> In this instance, your mythical tales and stories are not so far from ultimate reality–for the endless spirits comprising the totality of Me *are*, in a cosmic sense, My offspring.[11]

As Creator of the whole universe, Source is far too immense to inhabit a small physical vessel like a human being. If Source as a whole being tried to inhabit a physical body, it would instantly be transformed into pure Source Energy due to the extremely high vibration. So, in order to experience physical life, Source expanded its self-awareness outward as thought-forms that we perceive as Light Beings who could enter into any other thought-forms, including humans (see next chapter). We call those bits of Source self-awareness inside humans "souls." Inhabiting a human as a Light Being soul allows Source to experience everything the human does.

That is the entire purpose of souls—to be a part of Source able to experience all types of adventures in physical matter (see chapter 4). As souls, we literally serve as Source's arms and legs, to have physical experiences for Source. We are the body of Source. And, as its body, our job is to carry God/Source into everything we do.

3

What Am I?

You are way more than you think you are.

When you look in the mirror, what do you see? You see a human being. An inhabitant of Mother Earth. But is that really you? When your child dresses up in an ear of corn costume for the school play, does that mean he is a vegetable? Does an astronaut become an alien from outer space when she dons a space suit to work outside the space shuttle? Looks can be deceiving. Your true existence is not limited to what your human senses can perceive. "You" are not your body. It is something you wear in order to experience human life in much the same way the child wiggles into the corn costume to be in the play, or the NASA mission specialist steps into the space suit to protect her from the ravages of space travel. Yet there is an immensely important distinction. While the costumes are inanimate objects, your human host is very much alive and self-aware.

What are you then? And how can you possibly be "wearing" a living, breathing being as a costume? The simple answer I was given is that we are literally extensions of the Source's own Energy and self-awareness. That Energy is a constant flow away from and back to the Source but its vibration varies with distance. Some denser areas or slower vibrations appear from our perspective to be formed into beings. Yet what we perceive as a living being is ultimately nothing more than viewing one slice in time, or level of perspective, or point of attention we have focused on, within the vast continuous stream of consciousness/Energy of the Being I call Source.

Imagine that Source radiates Energy outward similar to how our Earth's sun radiates sunlight. Source Energy is a constant stream, not of light and heat as with sunlight, but of awareness and consciousness. And, though it is a never-ending, omnipresent stream of Source's life force, you can take a snapshot at any point along the way and capture or "fix" a level of perception or awareness. You would then perceive that snapshot or part of the consciousness stream, that level of perspective, to be a living *being*. And, just as you get a slightly different picture of your subject when you move your camera a little bit forward, backward, or side-to-side, moving the point at which you take a snapshot of Source Energy gives a different perspective on beings. Small movements produce only slightly different versions of the same type of being. Large movements disclose Energies you would identify as different types of beings from humans.

The human beingness you experience is a snapshot of awareness and perspective taken at one point—call it the Human Point—along the stream of Source self-awareness. From Source's perspective we remain firmly entrenched in its mind, its imagination, and its existence. From our perspective, humans are real beings. They appear to have existence separate and apart from the Source. That is our gift from Source. Humans come alive, as we use that term, just by virtue of the fact that we have focused our attention on the Human Point in the stream of Source Energy.

Move your camera a tiny bit to the left or right of where you are taking the Human Point snapshot and you see human beings with differing realities or levels of perspective. Some, for example, will see the glass half empty, while others see it as half full. Many will concentrate all attention upon themselves. A few will devote their lives to family or even humanity at large. Too many will suffer handicaps, as too few glory in athletic achievements. The realities of lives can vary greatly, though all are human.

Raising your camera sight closer to the Source than where you took the Human Point snapshot, however, begins to reveal an exciting change. The higher upstream, so to speak, we take the snapshot the more Source Energy and self-awareness reflects in the picture. The version of human being we see there might be called "enlightened." He/she has more Source awareness and begins to see the universe from a more global and sophisticated viewpoint. If we could swim upstream in Source's Energy flow and carry our cameras with us, we would reach a point where our snapshots would reveal Beings of Light or Energy like those I met. Or like the ones author Dannion Brinkley met when he died, as described in

Saved by the Light.[12] A Light Being just like I *became* after I died (see Chapter 21). Even higher levels of existence and awareness await us beyond the Light Being level. (Several are described in Part III as part of the narrative of my own beyond-death experience.)

In between where you took the Human Point snapshot and the Light Being photo are hundreds of levels of awareness and perspective we can explore while still in the body. Every little nudge in the direction of Source brings greater enlightenment. Enlightenment allows more understanding and a broader perspective on life. The broader the perspective you have the easier life is, because you see each event not as a huge crisis that may overwhelm you, but as a small blip on the screen of a full and rich life. In addition, the understanding that enlightenment brings helps keep our relationships in perspective. We become less dependent upon others for our happiness and fulfillment because we can increase them ourselves through the simple expedient of moving our perspective to higher positions on the Source Energy stream.

Of course, there actually is no linear sequence to Source's Energy flow. That analogy is used to simplify the explanation. Source Energy is everywhere all the time. It is in everything we perceive in our universe. Every being. Every non-being. Every molecule of everything. And everything in turn exists solely within the Source itself—when viewed from Source's ultimate perspective.

Now study the Human Point photo more closely. What you initially perceived, with human abilities and perspective, to be a discrete, individual human being now appears multi-dimensional. During my beyond-death experience I was astonished to experience a transition from the "self" I had known in the body through higher and higher levels of consciousness, each of which I remembered having lived before. Each one felt like the "real" me, only with far greater mental capacity, memory, and abilities as I progressed through the process. I understood at last that what we really are is a compilation of multiple levels of consciousness, each of which perceives itself to be a singular, unique person. Each has its own method of origin, lifespan, and innate nature.

The three levels I experienced, though stated here in reverse chronological order, are:

> Immortal Light Being. Eventually I transformed into the same Being of Light and Energy as those I met in the Light. I shared their abilities of mental telepathy, full access to Universal Knowledge, and "essence" merger. (See Chapter 21.)

> The part of the Light Being Energy that temporarily separates out to become the soul of a human being. I include this as a level of being because once out of the body I noticed my personality and abilities changed, even before full transition into Light Being status, making this a level of transition unlike the other two distinct beings described here. (See Chapter 20.)

> The soul-personality while temporarily blended with the human animal to form the combined being we call "human." This is the level we are currently living.

The one level we are *not*, however, is the human body. That is a separate being entirely.

Being of Light. First, and foremost, at your highest

vibrational level you are one tiny aspect of the Source's self-awareness—a Sourcebeam radiated outward far enough and slowed down enough to be fooled into believing you are someone other than the Source. I call that someone a "Being of Light," for that is how we looked during my beyond-death experience.

The Source did not *create* Light Beings in the sense that we are constructed of raw materials outside of and different from the Source. We were and are "created" by the Source by being individually *thought of* and recognized as something like "splinters," "droplets," "cells," or "points" of Source consciousness, similar to how your dream characters are mentally conceived as individual people. A Light Being is the Source's thought Energy congealed into a pool of self-awareness that we perceive to act like a being. This works in a way similar to how your dream characters behave as though they are not you even though they are just your own thoughts.

A Light Being is not truly a separate or different entity from the Source. Our creating Source conceptualized or manifested itself into extensions of self-awareness that could engage in individual experiences seemingly separate and apart from the whole of its entity. Source did this to partake of its own creativity and the wonders it had wrought in the universe. So billions of Light Being thought-forms proceeded out of Source and took up a form of artificial individuality for the pure joy of it—just to satisfy Source's overwhelming curiosity about itself. And to give Source, a solitary being, a way of interacting.

As Light Beings, we enjoy a wide range of awareness and evolutionary states, much as we are used to in human form. But we have dazzling superpowers at our disposal, including wordless communication that conveys "knowing" in a blend of knowledge and experience, and, the ability to literally merge our Energy totally into another Being and experience what it has lived over the eons it has witnessed.

In Light Being form, we continue our illusory separate lives, learning, and evolving ever higher in vibrational state. We incarnate over and over again into different human and other species' bodies, becoming what humans would perceive to be time travelers. And it is our own evolution that impels us to contrast and compare the present moment with all that has gone before and will come after. That is how we gain insight and grow from lifetime to lifetime.

Light Beings eventually achieve "knowing" that they are extensions of Source awareness and not separate beings. Once the illusion of separation is broken, that alone may cause a Light Being to dissolve back into Source, as nearly happened to me (Chapter 21).

You most likely are completely unaware of your Light Being level of existence. But that was your first identity in the mind of Source. And that is the identity you will resume after leaving this world upon the death of your host body.

Soul. Second, the individual "self" you currently do perceive is but one aspect or level of your own total Light Being consciousness. Like Source, and because you are just an extension of Source awareness, as Light Being, you can slow part of your Energy down low enough to fool yourself into believing part of you is someone else. And that slower vibration can be invested into physical matter. This Energy is what forms the soul of the human being you currently think you are.

You, in soul form, are not separate or different from you as Light Being. "Soul" is just part of your total Energy reduced in level of awareness enough to enjoy the illusion of being human—like a character in your dreams. Think about how you play different roles in your dreams, often acting in ways you would never consider while awake. Souls are a level of Light Being awareness cast into roles, like parts in a play, in which they perceive themselves to be humans. But they are not.

Souls continue their illusory separate lives, learning, and evolving ever higher in vibrational state until awakened into Light Being awareness after leaving the body. The soul's life cycle outside a body is short and rather limited. It can leave the body for short periods of time during sleep, sedation, or unconsciousness—what we call out-of-body travel. Ultimately, it leaves the body permanently to enter the Light and undergo the various stages of transition necessary for it to remember who and what it really is—part of you, an immortal Being of Light.

I discovered during my afterlife experience that the rest of my

Energy "stayed" at the Light Being level of existence while the soul component enjoyed its human adventure. This became obvious to me during the "rejoining" process, when my soul level of awareness dramatically expanded into memories of eons of living as many types of beings over thousands and thousands of Earth years, as well as into memory of all the Knowledge of the Universe. Once reunited with the totality of my Light Being Energy, the "soul" I once thought of as myself dissolved as a separate identity, taking into my Light Being form all of my experiences and data collected during this human life.

Souls are eternal to the same extent Source and Light Beings are eternal. And, when each soul has experienced what it chooses, it will awaken to its evolved Light Being splendor, and ultimately merge back into Source as a whole. Therefore, while the observable life of a human body has a beginning and an end, the soul inside has always existed as part of a Light Being extension of the Source.

To the Light Being, the part that becomes the soul of a human feels like it is asleep or unconscious, like your body's leg does when you sit on it too long. Thus the soul never actually *leaves* the Light Being or the Light while experiencing human life—only its level of awareness does. When this bubble of illusion burst for me, incredulity that I could have been so fooled about human life roared over me in tidal waves, nearly drowning me emotionally. No one had ever told me I am actually a magnificent, powerful Light Being. But I am. And so are you.

Part of the Human Being. Third, in soul form you are an indivisible part of the physical being you see in the mirror. Imagine Source to be like the sun and each of us to be an individual Sourcebeam. Just as sunshine is absorbed by the various forms of physical matter on Earth, we Sourcebeams can choose to be absorbed into any type of physical matter, including humans, in order to experience its life and process of evolution.

As Light Being Energy we can choose to enter into a human fetus as the soul and meld our personality with that of the developing human's. Thereafter, the body and soul operate as one living being we call "human." Yet there are still two personalities within that form, each vying for attention and experience. And the interplay produces astoundingly complex personalities.

Humans are very generous sentient animals that tolerate and accommodate being inhabited by another type of being composed of higher energy signatures—us. And, while humans are self-aware, they do not, in and of themselves, possess the level of Source self-awareness that we do. Their self-awareness revolves around knowledge that they are alive and can die, as well as recognition of their emotions and instincts.

We ourselves are not human. Humans are a species of animal, just like dogs, cats, horses, cows, etc., indigenous to planet Earth. *We* are not humans. We only inhabit them in order to see, hear, taste, touch, smell, and live as a human does.

This probably sounds like heresy to you. Religion has always taught that God made us in his own image, and most people assume that means a human image. We know humans are composed of flesh and blood. The next logical step is to assume that God created this flesh and blood form as a special, higher species of beings, a race unique in the entire universe. Only part of that belief is true, according to my excursion into Universal Knowledge. Humans are special and unique among all creatures in the universe, just as every part of Source's universe is special and unique. Yet humans are essentially Source thought-forms that vibrate so slowly they appear to be solid physical matter. And you are not a human. You are the spiritual being *inside* the human body.

The Light Being soul is not a physical organism that can be surgically removed from the host. In human parlance, in soul form we are completely infused throughout our human hosts as Energy, just like blood, water, DNA or other cellular components are. We separate from the body only voluntarily, such as upon imminent death of the host human being. And, unlike TV aliens, Light Being souls do not "take over" the human's life. We honor it and allow it to express itself.

As I understand it from the Light Being's perspective, human existence is an illusion of our own creation, much like dreams are an illusion of the human/soul combined being's creation. Both are *real* states of awareness. Both disappear when the illusion is broken. In the soul's case, the illusion dissolves when it processes far enough in the transition we call the afterlife to awaken to its full

Light Being nature. In the case of dreams, the illusion terminates abruptly upon the body's awakening to a more conscious state.

In sum, the following diagram depicts some of the multiple layers of awareness that constitute what we perceive as our existence:

> Source (extends awareness) → Light Being (extends awareness in soul form) → human life (extends awareness) → dreams

By nature, we enjoy unlimited layers of awareness beyond the above diagram. The important fact to understand about these multiple levels of awareness is that, just as we humans consider our dreams not to be "real," Light Beings consider human life not to be "real," and Source considers the entire universe to be only an extension of its own imagination and creativity. All of creation is in fact transpiring exclusively in Source's mind, just as our dreams transpire exclusively in our own minds. The façade of different beings evaporates once the basic truth that they are merely levels of Source self-awareness is glimpsed.

Our True Nature as Light Being Souls. Although we previously took a snapshot of Source's Energy flow and called it a Being of Light, it would be more accurate to acknowledge that in our Light Being forms we are actual components of Source than to continue thinking of ourselves as separate beings. We are literally part of Source in the same way a droplet of salt water on the beach is part of the ocean. Once a small bit of salty water separates from the ocean, we call it a "drop" of water instead of "ocean." Yet it is still part of the ocean with the exact same characteristics. Its composition is hydrogen, oxygen, chlorine, and other ocean chemicals. It still tastes salty like ocean water. The water drop's location on the beach does not change its nature.

In much the same manner we are small local "droplets" of one consciousness, one sentient intelligence that is eternal, universal and omnipotent–the Being we call "God." We feel like separate beings, but are in fact parts of God/Source's Energy field. So is everything else in our universe. A being's or thing's physical location within the universe does not change its innate nature. All matter collectively constitutes Source in the same way that all of the droplets of salty water collectively make up the ocean.

The only difference between the droplet of salty water and the Atlantic Ocean is volume, and therefore power. Similarly, the only difference between the Source and each of us is the amount of Energy, and therefore power, we have. In other words, our little bits of Source Energy are not strong enough to have all the power of the Source; we have reduced versions. Our relationship to Source is that our tiny little bits of Energy are *qualitatively the same*, but quantitatively less powerful.

At first, I found it incredible to accept that a Light Being still has the exact same composition and beingness as the Source, including intelligence, emotion, knowledge, and experience. The confirming explanation, however, rocked me like an explosion, a

Light Being also retains the dual nature of being *both* an individual point of Source awareness *and* an integral part of the Composite Being Source. Both exist simultaneously. They are but two different perspectives on one Being's multiple levels of self-awareness. Each Light Being—each of us—*retains its identity as the Source*, while simultaneously enjoying the opportunity to experience different types of existences as a discrete personality. This is exactly what Source intended. And it is a message we have heard from other authors:

> My divine purpose in dividing Me was to create sufficient parts of Me so that I could *know Myself experientially*. There is only one way for the Creator to know Itself experientially as the Creator, and that is to create. And so I gave to each of the countless parts of Me (to all of My spirit children) the *same power to create* which I have as the whole.
>
> *This is what your religions mean when they say that you were created in the "image and likeness of God." This doesn't mean, as some have suggested, that our physical bodies look alike (although God can adopt whatever physical form God chooses for a particular purpose). It does mean that our essence is the same. We are composed of the same stuff. We ARE the "same stuff"! With all the same properties and abilities—including the ability to create physical reality out of thin air.*[13]

This passage from *Conversations with God,* written two years after my afterlife experience, echoes my understanding that not only are we part and parcel of what constitutes Source, but we also have the same innate traits and abilities (though to a lesser degree).

Like Source, as Light Beings, we are both unified singular beings, *and* composite beings made up of several layers of awareness, of which the soul is but one. And in our pure soul state, after leaving the body and entering the Light, we incrementally abandon once-human habits and thought patterns to blossom into our natural personalities as eternal Beings. The first huge difference I personally noticed was the loss of fear and the myriad personality traits I exhibited as a human that were based upon and projections of that emotion. The second dramatic change was in the speed with which I could think, manifest physical matter, and absorb "knowings."

All this means that you and I—though as souls inside bodies we vibrate at a much slower frequency than when in full Light Being state—*have the same innate nature as Source.* Souls have the same multi-level perspective, the same access to Universal Knowledge, and the same ability to manifest reality. *We therefore have tremendous power!* Power we can harness even while in human form—if we so choose.

Light Being/soul powers include:

Dual Nature. Having dual natures is a basic character trait of Light Beings. When Light Beings are in their natural state, each maintains its ability to experience individuality, but it can also share all that it is with others. Simple attention and intention selects the predominating perception. And, both states can exist contemporaneously. We can perceive ourselves as individual beings while also merged into each other. This is the true nature of the Source, of which we are part.

The dichotomy of individuality/multiple-personhood was mine to enjoy briefly, while merged into five other Light Beings, as described in Chapter 21. Switching back and forth from being the single personality I have always known to living as part of a six-person merged being was exhilarating. What a rush, alternating between relishing my own "past" and "future" lives, and absorbing my friends' thoughts and emotions as they lived my just passed life on Earth! That wonder was topped only by the intrigue of temporarily living as though I were one of my Light Being friends. Imagine a virtual reality game where everything seems as real as this present moment in your own life—complete with familiar emotions—even though the events and emotions are *from another Being's life and experiences.*

There are no human words or constructs to accurately depict this multiple-personhood nature. A somewhat analogous existence might be what psychiatrists call multiple personality disorder. The split personality patient may lead two or more lives as seemingly different persons who are unknown to each other. The goal of therapy is to integrate them into one whole personality. It is ironic that we call this condition a mental illness. In a sense, we are all part of the Source's "mental illness" of separate personalities comprising a whole Supreme Being. The difference is Source is fully aware of each of its "personalities" while still enjoying its collective oneness. And, of course, Source is not mentally ill!

Souls are accustomed to living a dual (singular and merged) existence in their Light Being state. It thus seems natural to experience dual personalities while in human form. One is the personality of the human being; the other of the soul within. As soul, we may or may not be aware of our existence as part of a combined body/soul being, depending upon our degree of evolution. The human usually lacks awareness of the soul within until an effort is made to enlighten it. (See Part II.)

Access to Universal Knowledge. Another character trait of the Light Being/soul is the ability to access all of Universal Knowledge.

Have you ever had an idea just "pop" into your head when you were not even thinking about that subject? If the thought then pops out of your mouth, others might ask how you came to know it. You respond with a shoulder shrug, "I just know."

Have you noticed that people in different parts of the world sometimes make discoveries at the exact same time? An example hit the headlines on June 26, 2000, when the international Human Genome Project and a private group, Celera Genomics Corporation, announced simultaneously that each group had quite independently completed 90% of the sequencing of the human DNA genome. Simultaneous knowledge infusions like these happen because souls have unlimited access to Universal Knowledge by their very nature as Light Beings. The information comes to the body/soul in the form of "knowing," an instantaneous download triggered by attention and focus. Both DNA research groups focused on this data and apparently received "knowing" about it contemporaneously.

Some people say that brilliant ideas, or grand designs, come *through* them instead of *from* them. Highly evolved or religious people will often use this expression out of humility and respect for their supreme being. That motive is good and pure. However, it is misplaced, and perpetuates a myth about our existence. Moreover, it is true only in the most literal of senses. Wonderfully ingenious thoughts do come "through" the human being in the sense that human speech or writing is used to communicate the idea. But the idea actually comes directly from the Light Being serving as soul, not some other being, such as God, or from the universe at large in the sense that it is separate from the soul. Ideas the likes of which the human mind could never conceive come from you and me routinely because we are extensions of the all-knowing Source.

As Light Being souls, we are absolutely connected directly to the Source's knowledge base, what I call Universal Knowledge. It is not a tenuous connection. Not spiritual or ephemeral. It is a direct hardwired line to Source, in much the same way that the electricity in your home is a direct hardwired connection to the electric power plant. And the information that comes over that electrical line comes *from you*. It comes from that little part of Source that has been designated as your Light Being. It comes from the Universal

Knowledge database accessible to all of creation.

The failure of the best of us to take ownership of our soul's creations fosters the age-old misperception that we are separate from our Source. And we are not.

Ability to Manifest Reality. As undivided parts of Source we share its innate ability to manifest reality. We literally create our own physical world experience while in human form, as well as in Light Being form, or any other form we choose to take during the course of our evolution.

One of the many exciting aspects of my afterlife adventure was the discovery that I could instantly manifest any physical environment of my choice, just by thinking about it. After relishing the bliss of the Light for a while, I sequentially manifested a tunnel, with the proverbial light at the end; a verdant meadow with mountains in the background; and a hospital corridor leading to the surgical suite. Each different surrounding looked, felt, sounded, and smelled just as it would on Earth. Each was as real to me as the laptop computer, table, and chair presently supporting my efforts to write this manuscript—with one exception. I *knew* for a fact that I was not in a tunnel, a meadow, or a hospital corridor. Therefore, I *knew* for certain that I had created those realities out of pure thought. The word "manifested" came into my mind as the explanation. "Knowing" informed me that it is part of our very nature as Light Beings to be able to manifest physical reality through our thoughts, beliefs, and emotions.

Inasmuch as we are Light Beings in soul form, we still have the ability to manifest while invested in a human body. The results are just slowed down so much by the lower vibration of the human's energy signature that we do not recognize them as our manifestations. We manifest all the time, whether we are aware of it or not. We also manifest in concert with others, in and outside of human form. We co-create with them.

The most common and easily recognized form of manifesting in human life is dreaming. While the body sleeps, we continue to create experiences for ourselves through the process of focusing attention and intention on "I wonder what it would be like to . . . ." We then manufacture something like a movie to star in to feel that desired experience. The movie might be simply re-enacting snippets of the day's events to process and understand emotional reactions to them. Or a dream could take events and characters from daily life and rewrite the script to experience an alternate ending.

Manifesting in everyday life partly explains why several people can observe the same accident or crime and see slightly different events. They each manifest a version of events fueled by the complex interplay of soul intentions and body data input.

Naturally Curious, Loving, and Happy. Little children are perfect examples of our true emotional nature as Light Beings. They are curious about everything, from their own human bodies to the universe at large. Infants explore their hands, nose, and toes. Once children begin to talk, they may hound us with incessant questions about how the world works. And how many parents dread the age when their young ones constantly ask "why?" after the answer to every question. This curiosity opens young minds and souls to learning at an accelerated pace and volume. Our phrase that children "soak it up like a sponge" nods recognition of this fact. That curiosity is pure soul nature and comes from being part of Source.

Children love unconditionally and openly. Toddlers in particular live love to its fullest because their human personalities are still in the early formative stages and fear has yet to darken their perspectives. Their idyllic happiness reflects the wellspring of love within. We often wax nostalgic for the happiness of childhood, not realizing it is part of our very Light Being nature and therefore available to us always.

In sum, triple near-death experiencer, renowned NDE researcher, and author P.M.H. (Phyllis) Atwater succinctly answers the question, "who am I?" in these words:

> I truly am an immortal soul, an extension of The Divine, who temporarily resides within a carbon-based form of electromagnetic pulsations that produces a solid-appearing, visual overleaf of behavior patterns more commonly referred to as "a personality." Phyllis is a name given to my personality, my temporal self, but the real me is I AM. And what I AM everyone else is, for all of us are cells in The Greater Body, expressions of The One God.[14]

The Source, in an act of pure love and creativity, extended a facet of its consciousness to form you. You are the Light Being Source manifested in its own image. You flirt with individuality as well as multiple-personhood. You can focus your attention and intention upon any aspect of Universal Knowledge, and gain it through knowing. You manifest your own physical reality moment by moment, alone and in concert with others. Curiosity and evolutionary forces impel you to extend part of your own Light Being awareness to form the soul of a human being, and walk intimately with it through physical experiences.

4

✳ What Does God Expect of Me?

What does the Source expect of you? Nothing you do not do automatically.

Everything Source intends for your existence as a Light Being, and as the soul part of a human being, is inherent in your very nature. You instinctively do exactly what Source intends just by virtue of Light Being and human nature.

Source manifested us to feel an artificial sense of separation from itself, to experience all the wonders of the universe it created, and to have the challenge of evolving back to it through the struggle of experiencing various levels of consciousness and existence.

Artificial Sense of Separation. The purpose of manifesting our universe was to create an environment where Source could learn what is it like to have other entities with which to interact. Because we are miniature versions of Source itself, and have the same ability to satisfy our own curiosity through manifesting, we do the very same thing in various ways.

Some of us do it by writing books, plays, movies or software for virtual reality games, in which we create characters separate from ourselves to behave in ways we would not. Those characters, of course, are based upon a combination of the writer's own personality and traits lacking in, but of interest to, the writer. Others of us read the books, watch the plays and movies, and play the games to get a taste of other lives. We identify with the personality traits we share with the fictional characters and thereby imagine how we would feel and react as those characters. We often have genuine emotional responses to these works of fiction, evidence that we are experiencing them as real to some degree. But the work of art itself is but a manifestation of the author's creativity. The characters are not "real."

Many of us watch television and movies to live vicariously through the characters portrayed there. For an hour or more we can pretend to be someone else and see what it would be like. We forget who we are and get wrapped up in the on-screen adventures. It does not occur to us as we watch that all we are seeing is a pattern of dots on an electronic screen. The on-screen people and events are not "real."

And we all dream. Dreaming is a way of trying out other modes of behavior, other personalities, and other events through a version of ourselves that we believe cannot suffer the consequences of its behavior. We say and do things in dreams that we . . . well, would not dream of doing in "real" life. We watch characters that seem to be us, behaving in all kinds of forbidden ways, and wonder whether we are actually capable of such behavior after all. But the events never actually happened. Dream characters may have a basis in our human lives, but they are not "real."

These are all ways in which we create someone with whom to identify to experience an artificial separation from ourselves, a separate existence from ours. Just to see what it would be like.

Our existence as extensions of Source, or Sourcebeams, is our Creator's way of writing a book, or designing a virtual reality game, or dreaming. We are essentially characters, created so Source can live vicariously through us as though we are separate beings from it. We are not literally separate, however, any more than the author's book or movie is a separate creature from the author, or the dream characters are separate beings from us. All are essentially *thoughts*.

The Source gave extensions of its own self-awareness, Light Beings, the opportunity to invest some Energy into physical matter in the form of souls so that we would actually *feel* as though we are separate from Source. It is the grandest illusion of all time! We have in effect entered *into* the book, the movie, the dream, and are experiencing what seems to be a life separated from the Source in the same way fictional and dream characters seem to be living separate lives from their creators.

The illusion would not work, of course, were it not for the fact that human nature, by design, includes amnesia. The human body has two built-in limitations that restrict our ability to readily access knowledge of our inner Light Being, which itself has access to Universal Knowledge that it is not separate from Source.

The first human trait is amnesia. We have all experienced having a vivid dream and then forgetting it within seconds of waking. Mothers say that childbirth is the most excruciating pain they have ever endured; yet, that pain is forgotten soon after giving birth. And, no matter how hard we try, we cannot remember everything that has ever happened to us since birth. This type of amnesia is human nature. It serves to eliminate from conscious recall data that does not promote survival. And it is one of the reasons we choose to blend with human beings, for it gives us the thrill of learning the hard way.

The second human limitation that promotes the illusion of separation is denial. Have you ever seen a 200-pound person poured into clothes sized for a 120-pounder? Do you know someone who drinks too much but claims he does not? How many of us repeat the exact same mistakes in every single relationship we have ever had? The human capacity for denial is larger than its ego. It takes great effort, often with the help of a third person, such as a therapist or friend, for us to be aware of things about ourselves we do not wish to see. If we can so readily ignore such obvious physical and emotional traits, think how much easier it is to ignore higher levels of awareness.

We have amnesia about who we really are. And it is that wonderful gift that allows us to feel the artificial sense of separation that Source intended. We do it automatically, by design. We do not have to pretend. What Source expects of us in this regard has been built right into the process for us.

Experience the Universe. Source also manifested us so it could experience all the wonders of the universe it created. To Source, all experiences are valuable, regardless of content. It is only human nature that judges the experience, saying it is good or bad, healthy or unhealthy, holy or a sin. Source does not judge experiences, something I was surprised to rediscover during my beyond death adventure. We are the only judges.

Once Source has manifested a splinter of itself to experience artificial separateness, that Light Being controls what experiences it will have—not Source. Source's goal is to experience absolutely everything that it, or any part of it, can imagine. And, because all Energy ultimately returns to Source, there cannot be any true negative eternal consequences of any experience. That is why Source does not monitor our behavior, or tell us what to do. There truly is no *ultimate* downside to anything we choose to do because we eventually return to merged existence with Source automatically.

An immense Energy Field does not care whether we dance, play cards, eat meat, or steal money, for example. Nor does it have an interest in our sex lives, any more than the sun we orbit does. It is hard for us to understand this while in human form, because we almost never experience a love relationship on Earth that does not include elements of judgment and control. Perhaps Neale Donald Walsch explains Source nature in this regard more understandably in *Conversations with God*:

This is the grand illusion in which you have engaged: that God *cares* one way or the other what you do.

I do *not* care what you do, and that is hard for you to hear. Yet do you care what your children do when you send them out to play? Is it a matter of consequence to you whether they play tag, or hide and seek, or pretend? No, it is not, because you know they are perfectly safe. You have placed them in an environment which you consider friendly and very okay.

Of course, you will always hope that they do not *hurt* themselves. . . .

You will tell them, of course, which games are dangerous to play. But you cannot stop your children from doing dangerous things. Not always. Not forever. Not in every moment from now until death. It is the wise parent who knows this. Yet the parent never stops caring about the *outcome*. It is this dichotomy—not caring deeply about the process, but caring deeply about the result—that comes close to describing the dichotomy of God.

Yet God, in a sense, does not even care about the outcome. Not the *ultimate outcome*. This is because the ultimate outcome is assured.

And this is the second great illusion of man: that the outcome of life is in doubt.[15]

The fact that the Source has no interest in controlling our behavior is not to say that it does not love us and want us to have enriching lives. It cannot help but unconditionally love and accept us—no matter what we do—no matter WHAT we do—because Source *consists of all of us collectively!!!* And it is this truth—that we are literally a part of the Source—that assures our ultimate return to it. The outcome of life is not in doubt. There is only one place to go, and that is back to the Source from whence we came.

The Source does not judge our actions when we are blended with human nature. There is no need for judgment because the Source cannot choose among bits of itself, among souls, and accept some of its parts and not others. ALL of Source Energy, every single one of us, every piece of dirt, every wisp of cloud, every molecule of the universe, returns to the Source because it is an undivided *part of the Source*. The Source could no more refuse to accept part of itself back into the whole than dry air could refuse to accept a molecule of water that evaporates.

We need not fear the consequences of acting human—that is the very purpose of taking human form. We are not expected to act like saints, or Beings of Light, while living as humans. And there is nothing about human nature that is inherently evil or negative from the Source's perspective. "Good," "bad," and "evil" are entirely human judgments based upon uniquely human perspectives and experiences. These judgments are based in the fear inherent in human personality, as well as in learned knowledge of the consequences of past behaviors.

The Source and its Beings of Light have no concept of right and wrong, or good and evil. To us, all experience is acceptable and uncommonly interesting, as I discovered during my life review with my five Light Being friends. (See Chapter 21.) So your Light Being nature will not prevent you from having negative or hurtful experiences. The responsibility for behavior rests on the shoulders of the body/soul as a combined being. Multiple near-death experiencer Dannion Brinkley more recently received the same message from Universal Knowledge:

> Within the system of Universal Consciousness, there exists no mechanism for the discernment of what we call "right and wrong." Simply put, the Universe does not recognize the difference between light and dark, good and evil. Therefore, we must! And within each of us resides this innate knowing. We have come to this earth to master the proper execution of our spiritual wisdom. In the end, we will act as our own judge and jury.
>
> And there is only one measure by which we will judge ourselves: were we motivated by love.[16]

Nor does our Source dictate which acts are acceptable or unacceptable. There is no such thing as a sin against our Creator, according to what it disclosed to me as I was about to merge into it. There are no sins against Source; only "sins" against each other. We, in human form, have adopted codes of conduct for ourselves through religion or law to govern our interactions and maintain some semblance of peace. When we break the important elements of these rules, we sin against each other because we have broken our agreement with each other.

The downside consequences of our choices are all felt in our own emotional life, not only during this human adventure, but also through all "future" lives we enjoy as souls, until the emotion is resolved. It is a fundamental of life that we incorporate again and again into physical matter, such as human beings. Reincarnation is a fact. And, distressingly, all the emotional baggage accumulated during each physical lifetime comes packed aboard each new tiny babe's soul personality, to be sorted through time and time again, until all possible lessons have been learned and traumas healed.

Moreover, all behavior consequences will be relived from the perspective of all involved during the life review conducted after death. Now, if that does not sound so bad, remember that other Light Beings will be able to experience everything you have, including your humiliation while you observe your life's behavior through the lens of unconditional love. Just as I merged into my five Light Being friends (Chapter 21), you may merge with other Light Beings after death, all of whom will see, hear, and feel every insult, betrayal, lie, and stab in someone else's back. Then, when you ultimately merge back into the Source, it will accept all your lies, insults, and hatefulness, along with all the murders, rapes, child abuse and everything else humankind has done to itself—and will accept it all with unconditional love and curiosity. No judgment will be rendered. No punishment meted out. The punishment is the utter humiliation and guilt you will feel during your life review when all your secret and not-so-secret failings have been displayed for all to see, and your loving God/Source to experience firsthand.

More immediately, the unacceptable, unloving, hurtful, and downright insane things people do to each other create a living environment here on Earth flavored with the consequences of those choices. We live in a world dominated by fear of each other precisely because so many of us have chosen to behave in a manner that generates fear.

Often we question why God/Source would allow such evil things to happen. The answer I recall is that Source neither allows nor disallows choices made by its component Sourcebeams. Souls, as well as human animals, by their very nature as part of Source have the right to express their creativity. The right to choose. More than that, we have the ability to manifest reality, a talent manipulated by the human animal if not consciously exercised for the benefit of mankind by the soul. Source cannot, and would not, negate these aspects of its own nature as expressed through its component parts. In other words, regardless of how powerful Source may be, it cannot change its own nature. Every being must act in accordance with its own nature, even when the expression of that nature results in acts that humans perceive as evil.

Source has given us an environment teeming with potential adventures and experiences by design. Our mission is to enjoy those treasures and live life to the fullest. That is what Source intends for us. That is all that is expected of us.

Challenge of Human Co-Evolution. Darwin was correct in hypothesizing that the human species evolves, as does every other species manifested by Source. Light Beings likewise evolve by nature, and as part of the process of human evolution. The evolutionary path Light Beings follow is from the Source, through many different types of experiences, including human lives, and then back to be rejoined with the Source.

While human and Light Being soul vibrations co-exist, they influence each other. The soul's Energy speeds up human evolution and shortens its duration. Being in the body slows everything down enough that we souls can have linear experiences and enjoy the human perception of time passing. That allows us the sensation of growth and evolution at a slower human pace, through learning the consequences of behaviors.

Each of us has a very personal evolutionary path and only we can judge whether we are on it. During my life reviews I learned there are Light Beings whose job it is to help us evolve, to teach us how to select experiences in order to round out our education, and to be there for guidance when we need it. I call these "councils." Together, you and your council choose particular "lives" for you to experience in order to complete your perspectives on every aspect of humanness. For example, you may choose to "know" blindness, from the perspectives of being blind yourself, having a blind spouse, parenting a blind child, and working for the blind as your vocation in different human lives. Similarly, you may choose to know every aspect of a relationship with another specific Light Being, such as being that soul's human mother, father, brother, sister, grandparent, aunt, uncle, cousin, spouse, lover, boss, employee, etc. Obviously, it takes many human lifetimes to accommodate all these forms of relationship.

During my beyond-death experience, I received "knowing" that Light Beings believe they are evolving the human species by inhabiting them. Our intention is to be beneficial. The soul's learning curve often determines the type of life a human will lead. And, because the lives are entwined, the human personality will influence the types of situations serving as classrooms for the soul. Clearly this process affects the direction of human evolution. Thus, we Light Beings co-evolve with our human hosts. One view of the nature of that interdependent relationship, that I discovered years after my beyond-death experience, is well expressed by author Michael Newton, Ph.D., in his first book, *Journey of Souls: Case Studies of Life Between Lives*:

> Souls both give and receive mental gifts in life through a symbiosis of human brain cells and intelligent energy. Deep feelings generated by an eternal consciousness are conjoined with human emotion in the expression of one personality, which is as it should be. . . .
>
> Many great thinkers in history believed the soul can never be fully homogeneous with the human body and that humans have two intellects. I consider human ideas and imagination as emanating from the soul, which provides a catalyst for the human brain. How much reasoning power we would have without souls is impossible to know, but I feel that the attachment of souls to humans supplies us with insight and abstract thought. I view the souls as offering humans a qualitative reality, subject to conditions of heredity and environment.[17]

Furthermore, both human animal and soul behave according to

nature, as the Source designed them, when blending into one personality.

In sum, our sole responsibility to Source is to experience human life and carry those experiences back to Source when we are reunited with it. Our *soul* responsibility is to bring the Source's true nature, which is unconditional love and curiosity, to everything we do as we evolve our way back to Source.

5

* What is the Purpose of Life?

Why are we here on Earth? Because we choose to be.

My beyond-death experience reminded me that we choose to come to planet Earth, to inhabit human beings, partly to assist in evolving them as well as our own soul Energies to higher levels of awareness. It is a gift we give others and ourselves. In the words of the late Barbara R. Rommer, MD, a revered physician near-death experience researcher:

> We are here to learn, to teach, to make a positive difference, and to be of service to others. We are here to learn and practice unconditional love and forgiveness, and to reconnect with our Creator. We are not here to hurt others or ourselves. Life is a precious gift. We do not have a right to destroy it.
>
> These events [NDEs] teach us that every second of our lifetime involves a choice. We are in control. We are in dominion. We can choose to live a life of fear, void of meaning, being a victim, and not fulfilling our purpose, or we can learn from our experiences and those of others and choose to walk in light, fulfilling our purposes. Our journeys matter. This lifetime is not about earning points for a bigger reward, because we will all eventually get the same reward. We were all born with this universal knowledge, but somehow we have forgotten it along the way.[18]

A Light Being may choose to experience one lifetime, or many lives, or no lives in the "flesh," as we say. It can choose to slow down part of its Energy and dwell in human form, or that of other species sprinkled throughout the universe. Yes, humans are not the only ones we inhabit as souls, a truth that eluded me until I recaptured all my memories in the Light. Light Beings can choose to retain a higher vibration and experience a discrete "lifetime" as a being that has no solid matter as we know it, on planets and planes of existence where all energy vibrates at a very high level. It can choose to "stay Home" between lives, living and learning in community with others, or resting in the utter bliss of complete unity with Source and its quadrillions of reunited Sourcebeams. Thus, becoming human is a choice.

Souls who wish to incorporate with a human can literally preview what a particular life would be like before selecting it, without spoiling the surprise. Remember, everything that can ever be known or happen already exists in the Source as Universal Knowledge. So an individual soul can access that databank, pull up scenes from a human life, and watch them as though it were a videotape of *This is Your Life*. Previewing a life demonstrates whether it is likely to provide the opportunities for the lessons the Being of Light wishes to learn. It then selects the human parents who will conceive that life and enters a growing fetus to be born with it.

Combining with a human fetus is an extremely delicate process. Souls with less experience may not do it well, and may end up leaving the developing host. The result is spontaneous miscarriage if the fetus cannot survive the loss. The soul may well enter into the next embryo conceived by the same mother, so its "life" is not lost. More skilled Light Beings, those with more human lifetimes experience, may have no difficulty combining with the host embryo. Either way, the process is not instant. When the soul enters the fetus depends entirely on its skill and the timing of its decision to incarnate. So the human debate about when life begins turns out to be moot. Human animal life begins the moment sperm invades egg. But it is impossible to pick a uniform stage of development when the Light Being becomes the human's soul.

I was shocked to rediscover that in Light Being form we remember everything that happens during the life of the developing fetus! That is part of the reason for entering the host during formation. (The other reason, of course, is to give the fetus time to acclimate to being a host.) So everything you say and do to the pregnant mother goes directly into the soul's awareness and experience. Take care, then, for our assumption that the fetus does not understand what is going on is totally erroneous. The soul knows full well its human parents' attitudes toward their baby.

While here on Earth, we often beat ourselves up for not doing the "right thing" all the time, or for not knowing what to do every moment of our lives. Big decisions cripple us with guilt and fear; guilt for *wanting* an outcome that we might not think is "right" and fear that the consequences of our choice will be painful. We cling to the idea that our lives are planned, and then bravely face the impossible challenge of discerning whether we are on or off track. Our beliefs from organized religion may also layer a mandate that we do what our church leaders prescribe overtop all this strife.

All this self-torture is unnecessary. It is not our way.

The purpose of life here is so much simpler than you might imagine: to learn how to love unconditionally despite the difficulty of the circumstances. Beyond that, we are here simply to *enjoy* the benefits of a lifestyle very different from our own as Light Beings. Human life offers us the most unique gifts, each cherished by Light Beings because it is quite impossible in our home environment.

One Such Gift is Surprise. The simple potential of the unknown thrills us in our role as souls, for in our natural state *all* is known. Here, in human form, we can savor the deliciousness of the unknown. Simple attention and intention does not instantly bring us all the answers, as it does in our Light Being state. Oh, we can tap into our souls' access to the answers, but few people actually put forth the effort to do it. And fewer still *believe* what they hear. So we are free on Earth to go about our daily lives in complete and utter ignorance of what lies ahead. The physical limitations of the human brain block our universal perspective and prevent us from seeing in advance the ramifications of all possible choices. You and I are forced by circumstance to choose rather blindly. And that is the *whole point* of being here! Where's the surprise if you know beforehand how events will turn out?

Try to release your white-knuckled grip on the belief that you must find your purpose in life. Your purpose is simply to live—live as a human. The sheer burden of thinking that your choices are limited to those girding the highway of one true path deprives you of so much joy from the gift of surprise. Your choices are unlimited. All the time. In all respects. In fact, it is impossible to make a wrong choice—for having experiences, regardless of outcome, is why we are here in the first place. It is our Source's basic purpose in sending out its Sourcebeams of awareness. And no matter what we choose, we *will* return to the Source. It is our nature.

While still in Light Being form, you chose this particular human life, with its wealth of decision points, in order to experience certain aspects of interpersonal relationships. Not to make money. Not to get a good job. Not to go to the right school. Not to buy one house or another, in one town or another. You are seeking a much simpler "path," if you need to call it that. And you cannot miss your path. You cannot fail in your purpose. Your inner Light Being guidance will see to it that you encounter the circumstances needed to fulfill your goal. And, if your body's personality is too strong for you to take control long enough to do what you need to do this time, you will just reincarnate into another human life to secure the desired experience.

For example, you might be here for the sole, and soul, purpose of being available to love your daughter. Not to do anything

68

preordained, just to be witness to her evolution and say just the right thing at the right time to foster that growth. Fulfilling that purpose requires only that you give birth to that daughter and then be emotionally available to her when needed. Truly loving another is the highest goal we can achieve. The highest purpose. The rest of your lifetime on Earth may have no other purpose than for you to enjoy what it is like to be human. So enjoy.

Often we incarnate along with one or more of our closest Light Being friends. We may have agreed to play a particular role vis-à-vis another Light Being, such as my playing wife to your husband role in this life because last time we were in human form I was the husband and you were the wife. This is the origin of the concept of soul mates. If this is your goal, it will be impossible to miss finding the soul mate.[19] Our purpose or path, then, is to play out these roles, and we accomplish that through the normal course of married life. Nothing more is required of us.

Similarly, we may have agreed to switch roles for purposes of a specific event, such as, you betrayed me last time and this time I get to betray you–just to see what it is like. *Remember*, like our Source, we are insatiably curious. About everything. All the time. Regardless of how human society may judge us.

You may have agreed to play a small but dramatic part in another's life, such as being on the right street corner at the right time to see a man with a gun and yell "get down" to a stranger. That stranger may then grow up to bring about a successful government ban on handguns. It is quite possible that you will never know during human life that your primary goal in coming here was just that one moment. Perhaps time will rob you of the memory of that stranger, and you will not be able to connect your heroism to his rise in national fame.

You may wish to experience what it is like to be a gay man or a Black woman, or homeless, or just an average Joe in today's America. Or you may have chosen to experience betrayal or abandonment in all its forms, suffering that pain over and over throughout life no matter how hard you try to avoid it. If so, then your life's purpose is accomplished simply by experiencing how the kind of life you chose unfolds. There are no big expectations to be met. No Earth-shaking goals to reach. Nothing to beat yourself up about doing or not doing. The very fact that you are in a body is enough to fulfill your purpose here. Everything else is gravy, to be enjoyed as though it were a delicious sauce flavoring your life.

Some Light Beings choose a specific human life in order to bring an important message to their colleagues in the field. That message may be epic, like Mohammad's or Christ's, or it may be precious to only one soul, such as when my 4-year old friend told me that my deceased father is "ok now." *My* life's purpose is to be such a messenger. I have always believed myself to be a catalyst, destined to randomly say whatever I am prompted to say, to whomever, about whatever, rarely knowing whether it will affect that person's life. I am still doing it, here in this book. Only this time the gift of my beyond-death experience has provided the message.

To understand how little purpose one human life may have to us you have to remember who we really are: Beings of Light, not humans. Light Beings are eternal. We have no concept whatsoever of time; we live in the eternal now. For an eternal Being, eighty years of human existence is one second long. So it does not seem outrageous or ludicrous to combine with a human for its entire lifespan just to experience one simple aspect of a physical state of being, like not knowing everything. Add to that the fact that Light Beings can incarnate into humans many, many times, if desired, and the urgency of accomplishing everything in one human lifespan evaporates.

Please do not allow your human fear to convince you that you must control your life in accordance with some predestined game plan or true path. Our society, I believe, has this backwards. The Source does not have a grand scheme within which you and I have rigidly circumscribed roles. There is no such thing as fate. No master plan, other than the Source's intention to experience all there is to experience, to enjoy all of its creation. Source therefore does not impose restrictions on our choices of experiences. Free will is real. It is true. It is your birthright. In the words of a fellow near-death experiencer reporting in *Blessing in Disguise*:

Everyone's here for a different reason, whether it's to

make a mark to make a difference in the world, or to have lots of children, or maybe to teach someone else a lesson whether it's good or bad. Even bad people, like [Ted] Bundy, may have been sent here for that reason. I don't want to say that God would make someone evil, but I think He lets life take its course. I used to think how could there be a God if He lets all these evil things happen? Then, after I had the NDE, I thought maybe He doesn't make it happen but He just lets it happen. He lets life run its course for other people to learn so other people can understand pain, so they'll learn the reality of a forgiving God.[20]

The Source unconditionally loves us. There is nothing we can do to negate that. No deed is unforgivable. No act so despicable that Source love is withdrawn. You are free to choose to enjoy all that physical existence has to offer, including accepting the unknown.

Upon hearing this you may exclaim, "That can't be right! Life has to have more meaning than just for the Source's entertainment." You are correct. Every *second* of your life has meaning–to Source, to you as a soul, and to those Light Beings with whom you share your very existence via merger. You made a contract in coming here to learn a certain aspect of yourself, to play an agreed upon role, or to do something for another's benefit or your own. That commitment is important to you, as well as those Light Beings who are counting on you. When you leave this life, you will know whether you honored your commitment and will feel the joy or disappointment of your conduct during your life review. It is not true that the afterlife holds no negative experiences. As a Light Being, you will momentarily feel the success or failure of your mission, not because others will judge you, but because you hold yourself accountable.

You will judge yourself and how well you performed here by the only standard that Light Beings value: How true were you to your Light Being nature? How well did you show unconditional love? You will examine your every act and deed, not to judge whether you made a success of your life from the human perspective, or even to see if you made a mark on the world. Your only inquiry will be how well did I love and serve those who love me? How well did I express Source love within the challenge of living human life? If you are not happy with the answers, the worst thing that can happen is you will choose to incarnate into another human and come back here to try it again. Is that so bad?

Because your guiding principle is a simple one—unconditional love—you do not need to know beforehand what experiences you should choose. That feeling of wanting to know the future comes from fear of lack of control. The need for control is a human animal trait, part of the survival instinct. You yourself feel no such anxiety. So try to relax. It is impossible to completely know your own intentions for this life while still in the body. You have chosen human life partly to enjoy its gift of the unknown. Honor that choice. Accept the gift of not knowing.

In the meantime, Lighten up! Allow the Light of your true nature, your Light Being nature, to bring you the awareness of your immortality. Allow knowing the Source's love to come through to your human awareness level to reduce its fear of the unknown. Try to live each day as you did in childhood on Christmas mornings, knowing every package holds a wonderful surprise. If you can do this, you will manifest happier opportunities that allow you to fulfill your simple purpose here. Kacie, a near-death experiencer who came back into body in a hospital morgue, says this about how our lives are guided:

> All of this [her afterlife experience] has taught me that if you make a move in the direction you think you're supposed to go, and you're going in the right direction, then doors will open. When you're not going in the right direction, then spiritual guides will close doors around you to get you to look for the open ones to help steer you and nudge you in the right direction. I honestly believe that that's how the universe works.[21]

Relax and trust yourself. Accept that you may not know while in the body just what it is you are trying to accomplish here. Then all you have to do is open the gift of the unknown before you and enter into the joy of being human.

Human Form Also Grants the Gift of Growth. Our vibrational level as Light Beings is so fast it approaches that of Source itself, allowing us ultimately to blend back into Source when our wanderings are complete. That energy signature is far too high, however, to allow us to instantly meld with human animals. The process must be painstakingly slow, beginning before the human's birth, so that both species may gradually harmonize their vibrations into the symphony we call human beings. The combined musical note is higher than the animal's but much lower than the soul's natural vibration. Many of the soul's natural abilities are suppressed at this level. Chief among them is the ability to access memory of who we really are. But it is this wonderful gift of amnesia that allows us the freedom to learn, to grow, and to rediscover the truth again and again.

The gift of amnesia is one of the primary reasons Light Beings select humans to inhabit. Amnesia of our origin allows us to honestly *believe* the illusion that we are separated from the Source. And that separation bestows a level of creativity that only true freedom fosters.

We are free to manifest anything our imaginations can conceive without the anchor of knowing it is not real. You can believe life ends when the body dies, allowing you to live like there is no tomorrow, without the nagging truth that you are immortal staring you in the face. You can fantasize that your life is important, leading you to seek opportunities to change the world, something you might never do if secure in the knowledge that this is all an illusion anyway. We can live and love one another in ways that fumble and fail only because we cannot remember our natural state of unconditional love.

And we can learn! We can learn new facts, concepts, and ways of thinking only because we have amnesia of Universal Knowledge.

Learning can be such a joy. The thrill of a new scientific discovery would be impossible if we were still omnipotent. The tender triumph a mother feels when her child first learns the word "momma" would not be possible without the amnesia of human birth. And no one would celebrate the accomplishment of long hours of arduous study leading to proficiency were we all to use "knowing" to gain information. Growth opens the door to success. And you know how humans love the feeling of success.

The growth process brings us step-by-step over hundreds or thousands of "lifetimes," through the emotional conflicts caused by human fear to the opportunity to experience our true nature's unconditional love while still in the body. Achieving unconditional love while still in human form represents not only the pinnacle of success for the Light Being soul inside, but also a quantum leap forward in evolution of the human species itself. Human physiology will change to eliminate biological overreactions, such as the fight-or-flight response, to common stresses that present no real threat of physical harm. This will lighten the human burden considerably, granting peace to our host species. And that in itself is a worthwhile goal for any lifetime.

6

✳ Where is Heaven?

Where is Heaven? No "where." Heaven is not a place as humans use that word. It is the end result of a process, not a physical destination. I learned the hard way that the religious symbology I grew up with–St. Peter at the Pearly Gates, angels, and heavenly mansions–does not exist as our ultimate destination, because heaven is not a material world. What does exist, though, is infinitely more interesting and fulfilling.

What we have been calling Heaven is more like a state of being, a form of existence, or various states of mind. It is the state of spirit existing in our natural form as pure Energy and pure thought. It is a state of consciousness so vastly expanded from what we perceive while in human bodies that it is beyond human comprehension. The afterlife is a level of self-awareness as far above human consciousness as being fully awake in human form is above heavy sedation. And it is the unrestricted enjoyment of our Being of Light nature, including unconditional love always.

One innate Light Being characteristic magnified in heaven is the ability to instantly manifest "reality" with a single thought. Instantly enjoying your own manifestations could be your idea of

Heaven—literally making your own human dreams come true. You could manifest the most wonderful Earth-like comforts and joys you can imagine, and experience them at will for so long as you wished. That would be a very simple form of heavenly existence, though, for it mimics human life rather than moving on to more blissful spiritual levels of consciousness.

Many might feel heaven is simply sharing in the unconditional love and acceptance, the joy and bliss, of being so much closer in proximity to Source. Heaven is also the feeling of being *Home*, our true home, where love is completely fulfilling and unconditional. It is the constant enjoyment of a happiness surpassing any we experience in the body.

Some would find it heavenly just to be released from the pain and burdens of the body and its fearful personality. Others aspire to a heaven of emotional comforts and reunion with loved ones.

Heaven is all this and much, much more.

During my beyond-death experience, those closest to the vibrational level needed to merge back into Source appeared to me to be serving other Light Beings in their own evolution. Consequently, one could say heaven is loving service to others.

Ultimately, heaven is the state of knowing that we are literally part of Source, and with that knowledge once again achieving merger with Source. In the words of one beyond-death experiencer who has also been there:

If you keep going to the light, and I hate to use the word "I" again, but I went all the way to the Godhead. Boy, that's not even the right words, but anyway, I went to the place where I no longer exist as a separate entity. It's like a drop in the ocean. You are totally dissolved. There is no separate consciousness. There is a vastness, and you are dissolved in whatever words we use for the Godhead.[22]

We are, after all, just bits of Source Energy serving as extensions of its self-awareness. Eventually Source Energy will all work its way backwards to recombine with the whole. That is the final heaven.

My own personal experience of almost total dissolution back into Source was the most humbling and moving experience I have ever had, or could ever imagine. I realized then that I am literally part of the God I had been worshipping. Little me. Insignificant me. I am as much a part of the Source as any other part—as you are. And I sensed firsthand that Source loves itself so much, and loves that little spark of itself that became me so much, that it allowed me to go out and revel in this grandiose illusion of separate identity. It radiated me outward to live all these lives, to feel all these experiences, and to embrace all these loves just so that I could feel separate and special. Feel fulfilled and excited. And then Source brought me back into itself so that I might remember that I have never been alone. Never been separate. Life outside of Source is all a matter of illusion, manifestation. I returned to Source to be reassured that all those times I felt small and worthless and powerless were just an illusion, manifested just for me so that I could come back to Source and appreciate how much love it feels for me. How much power I really have. How incredibly spectacular we really are. Because I never would have appreciated those things without the comparison. The raw emotional power of that communion is too much to bear now that I am back in human form.

When we merge back into the Source as a Collective Being, we will know *through experience* all there is to know, to feel, to live, to create, and to love. We will know it from the perspectives of every other little Sourcebeam radiated outward to live its own separate illusory life away from Source. We will float in a tidal wave of experiences from which to choose, moment by moment. And we will know complete unity with all of creation.

The path to heaven is not paved with sacrifice and penance. It is constructed step-by-step through evolution back to the highest vibrational state, a state that will allow us to rejoin Source's Energy and dissolve back into it permanently. That evolution is accomplished by our conscious efforts to *be* and live our true nature as extensions of Source Energy; our attempts to experience unconditional love, happiness, and peace on a consistent basis despite the trials and tribulations of physical forms; and our accomplishments in relating to one another and ourselves in a way that expresses nonjudgmental acceptance. We must abandon the fears of human nature and learn to express our spiritual nature while in the body before we may move on to higher evolutionary states. The reward will be grander and grander heavens to enjoy when we leave this temporary human plane.

7

Where is Hell?

Where is Hell? There is no such place. "But hell does not exist as this *place* you have fantasized, where you burn in some everlasting fire, or exist in some state of everlasting torment," says God in Neale Donald Walsch's *Conversations with God.*[23] My own experience confirmed this.

One of the fundamental truths I recall from my beyond-death experience is that there is no "Hell" as we fear. As Light Beings who are part and parcel of the Source, we have only one place to go when we leave physical matter, back to a higher vibration closer to our Source.

Source is the Creator of all that exists in our universe, and all that exists is part of it. The Source has no reason to create a place to punish its own extensions of awareness that I call Light Beings. The sole purpose of our existence is so that Source can experience itself and its own creative manifestations. Nothing we do is unexpected by Source. It wishes to experience *every* facet of living in physical and nonphysical form, including all those acts humans deem evil or despicable. There is therefore no possibility of being judged undeserving of an openhearted unconditionally loving welcome Home with Source.

No soul goes to a place of damnation for all of eternity. No human body goes anywhere after death but back to the component chemical elements of which it is comprised.

That is not to say that Source avoids all unpleasant or hellish experiences. Individual souls may temporarily experience hellish adventures and states of being as part of their overall travels in quest of experiences of all types. Source understands that it cannot know true bliss until it is contrasted with true suffering. So we Light Beings experience both on its behalf.

Some near-death experiencers (NDErs) report trips to hell after they leave their bodies. My understanding of our nature as Light Beings leads me to believe that those NDErs may not have gone far enough through the transition from human to Being of Light to lose their combined human/soul personalities. So they manifested events born of human fear, as though they were still in the body.

Alternatively, these NDErs may consider the life review, with its associated emotions, to be a form of punishment expected only in hell. During a life review you feel every emotion you caused another to feel during human life. You will live it fully, intensely, and remorsefully if you cause another being pain. This is the only hell you will suffer when you leave this life, but it will be so much more humiliating because it will be a hell of your own creation. Yet it is temporary. All hellish or unpleasant events experienced after permanently leaving the body after its death are temporary, and last only so long as it takes you to come to terms with the end of your human adventure and make emotional peace with yourself.

There is no final place of suffering for all eternity. We spend eternity as we began it—as part of Source.

My exposure to Universal Knowledge likewise convinced me that there is no such being as the Devil. He (for the Devil is usually represented by a male figure) is a fiction created by early primitive humans frightened by traumas they observed in the world into seeking someone to blame other than a benevolent God.

The fact that humans judge some behaviors to be evil does not mean there exists a Devil who influences our choices. We are responsible for our own choices, our own thoughts, acts, and deeds. Only us. The desire to escape that responsibility may be human nature. Yet we cannot escape our true nature as Light Beings, who do take complete responsibility for not only our own actions but also their consequences.

The Source created all the matter in our universe. No one and no thing unloved proceeded out of Source.

8

✳ What is the True Religion?

There is no one true religion, only truth itself. Seek to know your own truth—the truth of the Source. You will recognize truth by its brilliant wrappings of unconditional love and acceptance of all of creation.

Do not confuse truth with religious dogma. Religion is a human creation limited to viewing life and death from the blended human/soul viewpoint, which is a minute portion of the available perspectives. And it is heavily influenced by human observation of physical matter. For example, intelligent, informed leaders in our world propagated the belief that the Earth is flat, based upon their detailed observations and studies of the known world. It was an accepted fact for many generations. This totally wrong conclusion was drawn in good faith from the limited planetary exploration known by historians and mapmakers of the time.

The same kind of human perspective pervades religious teachings. A more expansive frame of reference is required to understand and accept the broader wisdom of Universal Knowledge. The following analogies may explain the differences in these vantage points.

First analogy: Early on in my transition in the Light, I gained the insight that time is a fiction of human design. More importantly, I realized that we could never learn the truth about time while trapped in physical bodies. This is because the body, by its physical nature, is incapable of surpassing time conventions in order to study the universe from a broader perspective. In other words, one must get *out of body* in order to observe that time is irrelevant. The human view convinces the most brilliant scientists in all of history that time does indeed exist and applies to the universe at large. These learned, insightful, but ultimately erroneous scholars may devise eloquent scientific models for the development of the universe based upon human time conventions, but they are still limited to human perspective. Scientists will never truly understand that time does not exist as a universal constant, unless and until they leave their bodies, either literally or by intentionally accessing and accepting Universal Knowledge on this subject.

Second analogy: Imagine how the average fifteenth-century Italian, for example, would have processed the sudden unexplained appearance of an American Indian. Clearly, the Indian's physical condition and language would be beyond the Italian's comprehension of the world as observed from daily life in a small village. The Indian's dress and skin paintings alone might convince the Italian that the Indian was an apparition, perhaps an evil spirit from the underworld. One could even envision the Italian concluding that the Native American was the Devil, rather than a fellow human with a different culture.

The Italian would interpret his encounter with the Native American within the confines of the only framework he had, i.e., his religion and the world of his observations. His conclusion would be made in good faith, based, as it was, on the human instinct to categorize every unknown person as friend or foe. And, in this case, the Italian's personal worldly experience would provide no cues that the Indian is friend, while his religious training would offer a construct within which to place the stranger as a "devil" or "evil spirit." Though that conclusion would clearly be wrong, the Italian could not know that from his limited experience.

The human experience is like a box when we do not expand our awareness outside of it and into Universal Knowledge. Highly intelligent and careful scientists and scholars can study human nature and produce well thought-out detailed reports and conclusions about life, but they are basing their reasoning on what is inside the box. The most pious and religious men can pen volumes of poetic imagery about God and Heaven, yet still be describing only the inside top of a box if they use only human perspective. The only way to even see that the physical perspective is a box is to get outside of it. Think outside the box, as they say.

Just as scientists theorize about time from living within it, and the Italian from the Middle Ages might mistake an American Indian to be a demon, religions often see life and death from a purely human animal observation point. And, that approach is too narrow to allow us to grasp the greater truths of Universal

Knowledge, which transcend all human-created belief systems. We must think outside the box when it comes to religious and spiritual beliefs. Otherwise, as the two analogies above demonstrate, our very sound and well-intentioned thinking will lead us to very unsound conclusions about Source, ourselves, and how life should be lived. We could end up tying ourselves to beliefs generated from human animal fear, rather than by Source's love.

Some aspects of religions are heavily laced with human perceptions and fear. Some are not. This is how you can know whether messages come from Source or humans: Do they assure you of Source's unconditional love, or play on your fears? Source's messages and the fundamental truths disclosed through Universal Knowledge generate love, not fear. Fear is uniquely human in origin.

You, the soul, know that no human belief system out of the many competing for our attention can possibly be the lone doorway to Source. Seek those belief systems that resonate with you as soul. Use discernment and accept those messages, traditions, and religious observances that make your heart soar with love and empowerment.

Allow your religion to uplift you and others. Do not torture yourself with doubt over whether you have found the one true religion. Evolution by its nature results in reunification with Source, so no organized religion is actually necessary to "win" your way Home.

Part II – Applying the Lessons Learned

9

✳ Living a New Way of Thinking

While living as humans, we may have some misconceptions about the answers to our most fundamental spiritual questions. For example, we may have the following concepts backwards from their underlying realities in Universal Knowledge:

Many believe God is a male, human-like individual. Source is not human-like, but rather an enormous self-aware Energy field/being that manifests our universe. Source is not an "individual" that exists separate and apart from us. It is a Collective Being composed of us, and all of creation, as we are composed of its Energy.

Many of us on Earth believe Source to be a supervisory parental figure that controls everything that happens within our daily lives. In fact, Source extended us outwards as bits of its own self-awareness in order to experience the universe it created, and gave us complete control over what we experience. We truly have free will.

We believe we are separate individuals whose actions have no consequences beyond our narrow view of our lives. The truth is we are all only one being—the Source. And we are all connected as part of that being in the same way all the parts of a physical body are connected. Because of this, everything we do affects everyone else and the Source itself.

We believe our thoughts are private and have no power unless acted upon. Unfortunately for most of us, our thoughts *are* power. They manifest reality just by virtue of their formation. Not one single thought is private, because the reality created by each one affects everyone else within the Source.

Most of us believe we are human beings, i.e., that living in a human body is our primary, or only, form of existence. In fact, we are only *the soul part of* the human being. We are actually powerful Light Beings—extensions of the Source's self-awareness—who are blended with human animals as a very temporary part of our eternal existence.

We believe most of what we experience as our personality arises from the human body, that it is a blend of heredity and environment. I discovered that my total personality had been formed over eons of lives as humans and other beings, as well as time spent in Light Being form between physical lives—that my soul, not this body, constitutes my true identity.

We fear death and its end of our physical existence. The death of the human body actually releases us to awaken to our full Light Being state of expanded awareness, Universal Knowledge, wondrous talents, and ecstasy in the Light of Source's love.

Now, my challenge, and yours, is to live these new insights within a manmade culture and environment we have designed to be diametrically opposed to many of them. Though I have the comfort of certainty about my true nature because of my personal experience, I still struggle mightily to translate that knowledge into more evolved behavior here in the body. To my dismay, my magnificent life after death, even the transformation back into a pure Being of Light, did not magically make me an always unconditionally loving, emotionally mature, and kind human person. Knowing what unconditional love *is* does not make it easier to live it while in the body. I have encountered two major sources of trouble in this regard—myself, and others.

My own attempts to live within this new way of thinking have caused me much heartache at the hands of friends and colleagues who are doing nothing more than being their human selves. The external conflict is the same as the internal one: the clash played out in all our relationships between the inherent animal instincts of our bodies and our spiritual nature within.

It is not, and will not be, easy to change our old habitual ways of thinking and acting. Much as we must process the grief and loneliness of other major changes in our lives, we may have to grieve changes in our levels of awareness. It is hard to give up the comfy, cozy beliefs and ideas we have had for decades, perhaps through generations of our human families. We will mourn the loss of what is familiar and widely accepted. Yet the peace and serenity of higher levels of awareness will more than compensate for the illusions we have discarded as though they were toys from childhood.

Another challenge will be that our loved ones do not appreciate it when we change, especially if the changes result from new beliefs different than, or even opposite to, their own. After returning to the body I wanted my lifestyle to reflect my new understanding of our Light Being nature. Others mistook my actions as a condemnation of their own beliefs. I lost nearly all my friends and supporters—some because they saw my leaving the law firm as a betrayal, and others because I appeared weak and broken, when they had always counted on me to be strong. So began my reintroduction to the internal turmoil of dual human/soul existence. You may have a similar experience when you integrate new beliefs into your behavior.

Finally, old beliefs may plague you, as they once did me. I know for certain that Source holds all of creation in the highest regard, and loves it all with equal degrees of unconditional love and acceptance. It is all part of Source. Yet, back in human form, I still sometimes wanted to elevate mankind to a higher level of importance in the grand scheme of things, as I had been used to doing. Actual knowledge that humans are wonderful, intelligent, and capable beings, but no more important to creation than any other bit of matter, waged war with my ego's desire to be more important, as I had *assumed* I was before dying. How was I to reconcile these conflicting beliefs? On the one hand, recollections of Universal Knowledge haunted me. On the other, I had forty-three years of indoctrination in the belief that humans are the center of the universe.

The quandary of how to balance human and soul natures now that I was back in the body left me staggering through forests, trying to find trees. All I knew for certain was that my human life thus far, though judged successful from the material world viewpoint, seemed to me to be a miserable failure from a spiritual standpoint. Blindly I searched for the key dangling right before my eyes. I had temporarily forgotten that while being vacuumed back into the body I could feel others around me whispering in my mind, repeating over and over, "Love is all that truly matters." It seems my Light Being friends were throwing me a life preserver. But I had to learn the hard way how to use it as a lens to focus my attention and intention on how to live peacefully again in the body. The plan that worked for me, using all I had learned in the Light, appears in this Part II.

We can each reduce the strife within our relationships by enlightening ourselves. All our lives will improve immeasurably if we learn to allow more of our true nature as Light Beings to shine through our behavior. The steps for doing so include (1) understanding the fundamentals of Universal Knowledge described in Part I; (2) increasing our knowledge and level of awareness of the true natures of both body and soul; (3) learning to recognize whether a spiritual understanding or animal instinct is dictating our actions, and why; (4) learning the true meaning of unconditional love and applying it to our own bodies and to each other; (5) healing old wounds and hurt-based perspectives; and (6) practicing consciously choosing thoughts, words, and deeds that reflect unconditional love until they become habit.

10

Wake UP!

By now, you may understand that you are a Light Being soul sharing physical life with a human being. But what does that mean, in light of the Universal Knowledge concepts discussed in Part I? It means we need to redefine ourselves by waking up to the complexity of who we really are versus how we have been acting.

Our belief that we are human beings who have souls is backwards. We are in fact Light Being souls inhabiting human animal bodies. As such, our behavior choices are not limited to those inherent in human nature. Our Light Being nature makes us capable of multiple layers of awareness, a tool we can use to access our true nature and allow it to influence our behavior choices. It requires only greater self-knowledge, a willingness to allow that knowledge to inform our actions, and retraining our bodies to behave as we desire.

We are in fact Beings of Light and Love. We will wake up as such when our bodies die. The only reason we do not enjoy the bliss of our heritage while in the body is we allow its animal character to dominate. There is nothing inherently wrong with a human being acting solely from its animal nature. But for a Light

Being soul to do so is the equivalent of an eagle deciding to spend its life *walking* the Earth. Like a bird whose nature is to sing and soar, our true nature is to be loving and blissful. We have chosen to walk as Earth-bound eagles largely out of ignorance born of amnesia and habit. Both can be remedied.

We can shake off the amnesia by choosing to deliberately wake up to our true nature as Light Beings, now, while in the body. It is not necessary to wait until the afterlife. We can heal the body's, and our own, unresolved fears and pains and eliminate them as motivating factors through enlightenment and self-healing techniques. Each of us can break old habits and learn to sing and soar. How? By engaging the first of our Light Being talents—shifting among multiple levels of awareness—to access Universal Knowledge about our true nature. We start by focusing our *attention* on the topic of our dual natures and focusing our *intention* on bringing awareness of each into our daily consciousness.

Much work will have to be done at both body and soul levels. Why would a soul, an immortal spiritual being heretofore imagined to be perfect, need to be changed? Because I discovered that most of my personality and identity remained intact after death, meaning it was not the personality of the human body. Therefore, most of the personality change will have to take place at the soul level. Tens, hundreds, or thousands of lifetimes spent on Earth and elsewhere may have formed our personalities, though we rarely remember any of them consciously. What does persist, even now, from these other lives is the accumulated "baggage" of unhealed emotional traumas. Those traumas must be resolved and healed before lasting change will occur.

Change must also include the body, for its personality is formed largely by fear and instinct solidified into habits. We must break those habits that are harmful and lovingly retrain our bodies to engage in more generous and productive behaviors.

Personally, it has taken more than a decade of struggle for me to begin to integrate into daily life what it means to be a blend of mortal human and immortal Light Being trying to coexist peacefully in one body. It means being consciously aware of both natures, loving both, and trying to evolve body and soul as partners. It is a task worthy of our best efforts, not only for the peace it brings to this life, but also for the tremendous impact higher evolutionary states have on us once we awaken in the so-called afterlife.

Changing Perspective. Our innate Light Being ability to shift between and among multiple levels of perspective sounds more foreign than it actually is. We have all experienced it without labeling it so grandiosely. Think of it as stepping back to see the bigger picture.

There are at least three ways to shift your perspective, to broaden it beyond the narrow view that may first come to you out of habit or emotional pain. They are (1) obtain more information about the situation; (2) imagine possibilities that *could* apply to the situation, without knowing for certain whether they do; and (3) admit that you do not have all the information necessary to see the bigger picture, and accept that you cannot possibly know all that is going on behind the scenes.

A plot from the TV show *Bones* demonstrates how these three methods work. In one episode, the FBI asked forensic anthropologist Dr. Temperance Brennan to examine the bones of a young man found with two plane tickets to Paris and a rare coin in his pockets, to determine his identity and cause of death. The FBI investigation revealed the man had been murdered for his rare coin collection on his way to sell it. Dr. Brennan searched for the woman named on one of the plane tickets to tell her what had happened to the man she had known fifty years ago. She discovered the woman was black, had been pregnant at the time of the murder, and had ever since believed her lover had abandoned her in shame over his biracial family. She had lived all those years unmarried, bitter and lonely, raising her child alone.

Upon hearing from Dr. Brennan that her fiancé had tickets to Paris for himself and her, and had been murdered on his way to sell his coin collection to support his family, the woman's perspective changed dramatically. She finally understood what had happened and realized she had been wrong for fifty years. The infusion of new information about the situation disclosed how her bitterness had robbed her of the chance of marrying someone else as effectively as her fiancé had been robbed of his coins. The woman changed her perspective on her whole life through simple acceptance of previously unknown information. She stepped back and saw the bigger picture with the aid of more facts.

The woman could have accomplished the same dramatic difference in her life much earlier by using either of the other two methods of changing perspective. She could have refused fifty years ago to believe her fiancé would abandon her, and imagined, without knowing for certain, that only death would have kept him from her and his child. She could have reported him missing so his murder would have been discovered earlier. Or, the woman might have gently accepted in her heart that she would never know what had happened, but would make the best life she could for herself and her daughter. Either way, her bitter view of life would have changed.

Just about any distressing situation can be improved by a change in perspective, specifically by stepping back and viewing the problem in light of the bigger picture. You might not want to smack the fast-food server who spills Coke down your shirt if you knew he stumbled because his toe was broken but he could not afford to have it treated. Or perhaps you would not lash out at your child for dallying in getting dressed if you knew she dreaded wearing hand-me-downs to school, and being the brunt of cruel jokes that she was afraid to tell you about because she knew you could not afford more. And, maybe, you could forgive an inconsiderate lout if you could see life from his perspective.

Changing your mind from believing you are a humble human being to knowing that you are an incredible spiritual powerhouse works just the same way. You must broaden your perspective. The best way to do that—the way that will completely convince you—is by acquiring more information about your true nature. You must make acquaintance with yourself as a Light Being through the role you serve as soul.

Increase Soul Self-Awareness. Each of us feels that deeply held secret childhood belief that we are special. That we are unique. That we were born to accomplish more than what we seem able to bound to this fleshy encasement. That spark of knowledge is *you* trying to inform yourself of your true nature. Listen to it. We are special. We are unique. We are far more capable than we allow ourselves to be using only human talents and physical abilities. We are powerful Beings of Source Energy and it is time to acknowledge and act upon that basic truth.

Initial contact with yourself as soul may be accomplished through meditation, lucid dreaming, or some of the exercises described by Eckhart Tolle in his wonderful book *The Power of Now: A Guide to Spiritual Enlightenment.* Mr. Tolle describes the process of self-discovery in part as follows:

> When someone goes to the doctor and says, "I hear a voice in my head," he or she will most likely be sent to a psychiatrist. The fact is that, in a very similar way, virtually everyone hears a voice, or several voices, in their head all

the time: the involuntary thought processes that you don't realize you have the power to stop. Continuous monologues or dialogues.

. . . The voice comments, speculates, judges, compares, complains, likes, dislikes, and so on. The voice isn't necessarily relevant to the situation you find yourself in at the time; it may be reviving the recent or distant past or rehearsing or imagining possible future situations. Here it often imagines things going wrong and negative outcomes; this is called worry. . . .

The good news is that you *can* free yourself from your mind. This is the only true liberation. You can take the first step right now. Start listening to the voice in your head as often as you can. Pay particular attention to any repetitive thought patterns, those old gramophone records that have been playing in your head perhaps for many years. This is what I mean by "watching the thinker," which is another way of saying: listen to the voice in your head, *be* there as the witnessing presence.

. . . You'll soon realize: *there* is the voice, and here *I am* listening to it, watching it. This *I am* realization, this sense of your own presence, is not a thought. It arises from beyond the mind.

So when you listen to a thought, you are aware not only of the thought but also of yourself as the witness of the thought. A new dimension of consciousness has come in. As you listen to the thought, you feel a conscious presence—your deeper self—behind or underneath the thought, as it were.[24]

The part of you that says "I am" is pure Being of Light–the splinter of self-awareness extended out by Source to experience life in the flesh. The "thinker" is the blended personality of human animal and amnesiac soul, both marinated in animal fear and survival instincts and spiced with unresolved emotional issues of other lives. The fact that you can identify both within yourself is proof not only of your dual nature, but also of your Light Being ability to hold simultaneous levels of awareness.

Quieting the thinker, and allowing yourself as Light Being to speak, will increase your awareness and enlightenment. Mr. Tolle explains:

> When a thought subsides, you experience a discontinuity in the mental stream—a gap of "no-mind." At first, the gaps will be short, a few seconds perhaps, but gradually they will become longer. When these gaps occur, you feel a certain stillness and peace inside you. This is the beginning of your natural state of felt oneness with Being, which is usually obscured by the mind. With practice, the sense of stillness and peace will deepen. In fact, there is no end to its depth. You will also feel a subtle emanation of joy arising from deep within: the joy of Being. . . .
>
> Instead of "watching the thinker," you can also create a gap in the mind stream simply by directing the focus of your attention into the Now. Just become intensely conscious of the present moment. This is a deeply satisfying thing to do. In this way, you draw consciousness away from mind activity and create a gap of no-mind in which you are highly alert and aware but not thinking. This is the essence of meditation.[25]

Dwelling on the present moment–living in the now–will position you to awaken to your Light Being nature. Author Michael Brown, writing in *The Presence Process: A Healing Journey Into Present Moment Awareness,* brings us the same message:

As the years unfolded, I began to develop an increasingly powerful personal relationship with what I now call my Inner Presence. I became aware that present moment awareness is not only a *state* of being; it *is a Being.* Present moment awareness is, indeed, "a Presence." The Being and the state of Being have revealed themselves to me to be One and the same.[26]

Shutting the conscious mind off and becoming aware of the present moment can be done with practice through meditation, relaxation, prayer, or sleep. *The Power of Now* and *The Presence Process* provide step-by-step guidelines on how to bring yourself to higher levels of awareness. Engaging your mind in awareness-focused activities, like reading spiritual and metaphysical books, can increase its receptiveness. So too can discussing spiritual topics. Read and reread the first part of this book to reinforce the positive messages found there and meditate on them.

Learn the truth of your dual nature. Prove it to yourself. As you observe your "thinker's" thoughts, notice them. No matter how hard you try to keep your mind a blank, thoughts will wander in. Try to characterize those thoughts that intrude routinely. Listen to them. Are they worries about what could happen? Or does your thinker rehash events that have already happened? How much of your thinking is devoted to fear of one type or another? How many thoughts go to listing the many things you have to do for work or family? You may find your thoughts to be typically consumed with one physical task or another. Yet the fact that you can observe those thoughts from another perspective, one able to objectively categorize them, proves the duality of your consciousness.

Stop the "thinker's" musings as they float into mental view. Empty your mind of all human cares. Let them go. Keep your mind open for another voice once familiar and now nearly forgotten. Listen. Mentally turn your eyes around to see inside yourself.

As you learn to discard routine thoughts and focus inward, insights may begin to "pop" into your mind. Glimmers of understanding. Maybe only one insight in a great while at first. You might not even be certain whether it is the voice of your thinker, or you as Light Being. There is a way to tell. Remember, the thinker tends to focus on routine aspects of human life. Light Beings focus more on concepts and knowledge—things you might label as philosophical, psychological, emotional, spiritual, intuition, or simply wisdom. You can tell your Light Being's thoughts by their "knowing" quality. You just know something without having thought it through logically. You will also feel certain the insight is the truth, with a calmness and clarity unknown while listening to your thinker's frantic voice.

At first, it will be easy to confuse "knowing" with fear. If you feel fear *while* the thought is forming, it is probably your thinker's voice expressing anxiety over one human life situation or another. You will feel resigned and accepting of "knowing" from your spiritual self while it comes to you, even though that knowing later causes you to feel fear. For example, if the thought, "what if I have cancer?" chills your heart, it most likely is your thinker expressing survival fear. If, instead, the thought enters calmly and certainly such as, "I have cancer," and thereafter that knowledge arouses your body's fear, it is time to consider that the insight might be "knowing" obtained from you as Light Being having access to Universal Knowledge.

Eventually, you will begin to recognize your Light Being voice as calmer, less concerned with activities of daily living, and more loving and serene than the one you normally hear in your head. It will emphasize less what you should *do*, and more who you *are*. Its thoughts will be wiser, from a broader perspective, and will reflect what you will recognize as truth. The more you practice listening for your Light Being voice the more you will hear it.

Information that comes to you through "knowing," or through meditation, might seem more in the nature of a feeling or belief rather than actual words you hear in your mind's voice. For example, you might suddenly know that your grandfather who is in the hospital with a heart attack will be fine. You may not be able to define "fine," and you certainly cannot explain how you know it. But you have a calmness and peace surrounding the concept of your grandfather's hospitalization. Or, you might know that even though your daughter has yet to meet the man she will marry, she will bear your grandchildren. Perhaps you cannot articulate even to yourself your sense of "knowing" about your daughter or her children. It may present itself simply as a feeling that her life will unfold in a way that is perfect for her.

Some of what your Light Being voice tells you may sound critical or judging. Do not be concerned, for it is not condemnation you hear. As a Light Being, you analyze every aspect of the human adventure, to speculate on how it could have been done differently, and to test behavior against your predetermined mission or growth plan. When we return to the Light, we use the benefits of total recall, the ability to feel others' emotions intimately, and multiple levels of awareness and perspective to study our own behavior. So do not let anyone tell you that you analyze too much. Do analyze your own conduct, and that of those with whom you interact, to see whether unconditional love is at work—or fear. Remember, the lens through which we must focus our attention is, "Love is all that truly matters." Your inner voice is trying to help you see yourself honestly through that lens, which might arouse your human defense mechanisms.

Continue to get to know yourself—you as the soul personality and the combined human/soul personality—outside of meditation. Listen to what others say about you and consider objectively whether it may be true. Ask loved ones, friends, acquaintances, a therapist, or anyone who relates to you honestly, to tell you about yourself from their perspective. Pretend it is a mini life review, where you can actually get into the other person's shoes and see yourself through their eyes. Feel what you have caused them to feel. That will help strip off the patina of denial you have been wearing to protect yourself from viewpoints that conflict with your own. And it will identify growth lessons to be learned.

Familiarize yourself with Light Being traits by reading and rereading Chapter 3, as well as the next chapter. Try to recognize your Light Being innate nature embedded in the insights you receive through meditation or from others.

Learn from your past behavior. Correct your mistakes next time. Grow. Evolve. Keep your lens of unconditional love in hand and try to view everything through it, including your own growth. You will be so grateful you have done this work when you come face to face with yourself in your after-death life review, for *trying* will count as much as succeeding when you judge your own behavior.

Increase Awareness of Human Animal Nature. Humans are the most wonderful creatures. Human nature includes wild extremes as well as stolid inertia. Both reflect the human's core animal nature, i.e., to survive at all costs.

Human beings are the most incredibly resilient creatures on Earth. They survive, and even thrive, in extremes of heat and cold. They endure the extremes of altitude, from a crushing depth below sea level to a dizzying height high in the atmosphere. Humans weather all types of weather. We find them outliving hurricanes, floods, avalanches, droughts, sand storms, and more. Humans can survive large quantities of radiation. They survive burns over large portions of their bodies, mutilation and amputation of all limbs, loss of multiple internal organs, illnesses that ravage their appearances and bodily functions, and even near-death experiences. Few other animals on Earth can survive the extremes humans do.

Humans are also unimaginably adaptive. They adapt to extremes of light and darkness, such as life at the poles requires. They can function on minimal amounts of water, food, sunshine, and sleep. Once having adapted to an environment or set of conditions, however, they often become immovable objects. We see this every day among those who devote their lives to maintaining the status quo. Yet this very adaptability and tendency to form habits is precisely what allows us to retrain ourselves to live as Light Being souls inhabiting a human body rather than as animals.

Unfortunately, the same adaptability that contributes to survival of the species also renders humans malleable by emotional and physical abuse into long-term victims. The body is so adaptable it can be trained to repetitively suffer most anything, including things that at first feel painful, destructive, or distasteful. For example, a woman who would find sex with a stranger repulsive can become a prostitute when necessary because the human body will eventually deaden or desensitize itself to the disgust. In the same way, a soldier who might throw up and have nightmares the first time he kills another will eventually adapt to it and be able to continue to wage war by becoming desensitized to the emotional trauma of taking another's life. This is the mechanism behind all destructive behavior, including overeating, overdrinking, and engaging in extreme sports or dangerous activity without appropriate safeguards or protection. Eventually the human body will desensitize itself to its own emotions and reactions in the same way the sense of smell becomes desensitized to an odor after we smell it for a period of time.

Humans have wonderful traits of passion, self-discipline (usually in the form of habit), protection of mates and offspring, and sense of community. On the other hand, human personality contributes the emotions of fear, competitiveness, and the will to dominate others. These human traits are foreign and opposite to those of Light Beings.

Some believe the human body to be merely a vessel for the soul and that it has no life force or personality of its own. This is the "temple of the Holy Spirit" concept. Actually, that is not the case according to what I personally experienced by dying. Humans are not empty shells. Nor are they merely physical projections of the Light Being soul within, as some propose. Humans are a species of animal designed to inhabit Earth who allow us to inhabit them. We therefore have an enormous responsibility for their welfare. And we must honor our bodies for the opportunity they provide us as well as for being wonderful beings in their own right. Light Being souls blend into human lives for the purpose of enriching them and evolving the species, not to debase them. Not to kill them, or slowly poison them with drugs, alcohol, medications and chemical pollutants. Learn to think of your body not as a possession but as a loving, generous companion whose welfare has been entrusted to your care.

It is important to learn which thoughts come from the body, from the human's personality. That awareness comes from *listening* to the *body*, not the thinker in the mind.

The body tells us what it needs for survival in very simple, direct ways. When it lacks sufficient oxygen, the body gasps for air. Hunger and thirst cravings drive the body to eat and drink, just as the instinct to propagate the species stirs in its loins. Maternal instinct floods mothers with overwhelming love and self-sacrifice for offspring. The desire to communicate with others produces gestures and utterances in an effort to be understood. The need for human touch brings the newborn's hand up to its parents'. In the same way, all humans instinctively seek out a loved one's embrace when they hurt.

The body alerts us when something is not right for it. All strong emotions trigger physical reactions, including hormone output and seemingly instant behavior responses felt in the body. Threats to safety churn our insides with a potpourri of chemical reactions easily recognizable to us as increased heart rate, sweaty palms, and the tingling of adrenaline rush. Long term, slow smoldering emotions like anger and guilt are often internalized into physical ailments. We might get a stomachache, headache, muscle tightness, or some other cue that our body uses to let us know we are ignoring emotions. Chronic conditions, like back pain and weight gain, may also indicate long-term denial of emotional reactions, especially unresolved pain. These ailments and physical pain are messages in the only language the body knows. Our job is to listen despite our fear or pain. As stated in *The Presence Process*:

> From the moment we enter this world, we are taught by example of others to fear and therefore resist pain and discomfort by controlling it, sedating it, distracting ourselves from it, numbing, it drugging it, and even going so far as to cutting it out. By the examples of others, we are led to believe that pain and discomfort are enemies and that when they manifest in our experience, we must escape or conquer them at all costs. We are led to assume that pain and discomfort are always indicators that *something is wrong*. In this world, it is very rare that we are invited or encouraged to respond to our experiences of pain and discomfort by listening to them instead of running from them.
>
> During the Presence Process, we are asked to consider the possibility that the experience of pain and discomfort is deliberate and therefore on purpose. In other words, when these experiences occur to us, it is because they are supposed to happen. We are asked to open our mind to the idea that pain and discomfort are essential forms of communication that have a necessary and valuable function in our life experience. We are being invited to change our perception of what pain and discomfort are and what the nature of our relationship is to them.[27]

The body speaks its truths as designed by nature, a language of sensations and physical reactions that can be accessed through a process called "somatic experiencing."[28] The thinker puts words to those bodily messages and plays them in our mind's voice. The voice may be sweet and simple, "I'm hungry," or, it can be complicated by years of emotion left unsettled. You know those messages—the ones that sound something like, "that b-----d isn't taking the last hot dog if I can help it." Clearly, the latter message reeks of emotion unrelated to the desire for a hot dog. Emotion that hints of pain long left unresolved.

Years of human life, perhaps hundreds of such lives, impact our soul personality, flooding it with all manner of unresolved hurts bobbing as flotsam and jetsam to catch in our thinker's consciousness. Sometimes it seems a whole city of thoughts have been built atop these pieces of floating debris, exaggerating their appearance so much we cannot see the little plank of a hurt underneath. It is our job now, as part of our awakening, to peer into the thinker's underlying motivations to discover the body's message and its simple, natural origin.

You have probably heard the saying, "Trust your gut." That advice may or may not be appropriate depending upon how your gut has been trained to date. Remember how as a child you had to learn to recognize the signs for needing to use the bathroom, and train the body to wait until you got there? Well, your body similarly has to be trained to give you honest messages unadulterated by years of adaptation to abuse or the emotional baggage that the combined body/soul's personality carries around. We should not base our decisions on what the gut tells us to do if it has not been properly trained.

For example, it may feel right to call someone who has hurt your feelings and blast them with every cruel thing you can think of to say to them. That may take the knot out of your stomach, but it does nothing but harm both parties' evolution. If you are inclined toward behavior like that, it is a good sign you need to retrain your gut. Only then will it be able to honestly tell you when you are experiencing a current (and not historical) emotion, instinct, or animal drive, and which one it is. In this example the original honest emotion is hurt, not anger, and the appropriate behavior would have been to discuss your hurt feelings with the other person, rather than seeking revenge through hurting him/her back.

Waking up to the dual being we really are is a process, one that unfolds gradually when we leave the body and transition back to our true nature in the Light. It will have to be a gradual process in human form as well. Give that process time. An excellent gentle awakening program flows through the pages of *The Presence Process* by Michael Brown.[29] You may find other guides as well.

Allow yourself to awaken step by step, just as you would in the Light, so you can enjoy the wonder of each stage of enlightenment. Yet keep in mind that when you awaken while still in the body, unlike awakening in the Light, you must consider the impact of that spiritual journey on your host body. Allow your human personality to get accustomed to the idea that you are in there, that an eternal Light Being soul *knowingly* inhabits it. Form a "knowing" partnership with your body whereby you begin to appreciate and honor his/her nature as you discover and honor your own immortal nature.

Awaken to your duality. Study it. Enjoy it. Live with it every day, for intimate knowledge of a being brings understanding. Understanding begets compassion. And compassion is the heart of unconditional love, our path back to the Source.

Fear and pain have dominated our experience on Earth over the epochs simply because we have allowed human animal nature to guide our lives largely according to survival instincts. But that need not continue to be the case. Each of us can, and must, evolve within our dual human/soul natures. Evolution of both beings will transport mankind from predominantly animal fear-based thoughts and behaviors, to a more peaceful existence enlightened by our innate unconditional love and natural bliss—a serene Earthly existence revealed to me to be the Third Epoch. To get there, we must collectively swing the pendulum back from the current version of man dominated by animal drives, the lowest form of existence for this blended being, to one capable of living up to the Light Being potential within. The tools are very simple and well within our grasp. In fact, they have been inside us all along. We need only bring ourselves to an awareness of the duality of our existence and learn to love and appreciate both beings, body and soul. That awareness and love will flow through us naturally once we open ourselves up to our true Light Being nature.

11

Who's In Charge?

You and your human host are engaged in a perpetual tug-of-war for control over the thinker, or whatever you wish to call that part of us that talks us into trouble. Anyone can function as either an energetic, intelligent, loving, knowledgeable, and evolved person, if their Light Being personality predominates; or as a slowed down, restricted, repressed spiritual being inhabiting a body driven by animal instincts, if the human's personality predominates. Most of us fall somewhere in between, though far too often we allow human motives to dominate and influence our thoughts and behavior.

Human thinking tends to reflect animal instincts of survival and propagation of the species, centering on tasks to be performed, scheduling, work, how to meet physical needs, and interactions with other people. Those who generally allow their human personality to control their lives typically attend only to animal behaviors like eating, sleeping, working to secure shelter and nesting materials, recreation, procreation, and avoiding injury.

Most of us do not allow our Light Being level of awareness to control much of our thinking, though it is possible. A Light Being's thoughts tend to be more spiritual, curious, creative, and reverent toward all of creation. People who allow their Light Being personality to control their lives generally engage in behaviors above and beyond an animal's, including having a spiritual life (that may or may not include religion), an intellectual life encompassing reading and discussion of ideas, a life of service to others that could be a chosen field of work or charity work, and an ethic that values all of creation and causes the body/soul being to strive to be a better person.

Where does the soul fit in? Between the two. The soul is the part of your total Energy destined to experience a blend of human being and Light Being natures. It is the workhorse of life, the part of you that trudges from lifetime to lifetime, and all points in between, collecting experiences for Source as you evolve your way back to it. Not all the good Light Being personality traits are apparent in the soul, however, because of the impact of its journeys through multiple human and other physical lives. Consequently, following the soul's choice will not always be best for both human and spiritual natures. Similarly, not all the bad traits are in the human. Both personalities are well rounded, and have good and bad traits, from a human judgment perspective. Each offers us its own wisdom.

Your natural curiosity and lust for life as a Being of Light soul knows no bounds. And because instinctively you know, on the spiritual level, that you cannot be harmed, when you as soul are allowed to take unbridled control you can be reckless with the body, and engage in behaviors human society adjudges to be wrong or evil, particularly if you are relatively new to human experience. The human personality must temper your drive for new experiences with an understanding of the body's limitations. For example, a soul longing for a reprise from the weight of physical matter may wish to jump off a cliff to regain weightlessness for even a brief moment. As pure Energy, the soul knows for certain it cannot die. So human survival instinct must intervene to prevent the body's demise. Similarly, there are some souls, who, because they are very unevolved and want to experience absolutely everything, come here and murder other humans. Once again, the animal wisdom that murder contravenes the survival instinct should be heeded.

Yet fairness dictates that the responsibility for avoiding harmful conduct should not be borne solely by human nature. The combined personality must be trained to exercise judgment and restraint *from the perspective of both natures* for the sake of longevity of the union.

How do we know which personality is controlling us at any given moment? By being aware of their primary motivations. I have spent many, many hours these past twelve years trying to determine precisely which behaviors can be attributed to the human and which to the soul without much success. Often the combined personalities drive behavior, so it is impossible to credit, or discredit, one or the other. I do, however, recall some defining characteristics from my·experience as a Being of Light during my 1994 death experience that we can use as benchmarks against which to study our own motivations.

A side-by-side comparison of the two natures reveals what I recall to be their most distinctive features and motivations that are opposites of each other. In other words, these human behaviors are "backwards" from Light Being nature:

Human fear-based behaviors	Light Being character trait
controls others and the environment	accepts others and nature as is
anxious over one's place in the hierarchy, competitive	understands there is no hierarchy, all are equal, feels no need to compete
fears the unknown, resists change	accepts that change is inherent in evolution

Self-interest based behaviors	Light Being character trait
self-centered	"whole" or Oneness centered
refuses to accept responsibility for one's own thoughts and deeds	knows every thought and act has repercussions throughout creation, so manifests carefully and consciously
no interest in learning, growth	curious about all of life
judgmental	non-judging and compassionate

| childish, emotionally immature | adult-like, with emotional stability from hundreds of lifetimes |
| ego-centered, or driven toward self-aggrandizement | motivated by what is best for all because we are all One |

Whenever you observe yourself or another engaging in behaviors from the left-hand column, you can be relatively certain that the human animal is, or has been, in control of the combined being's thoughts and behaviors. I say "has been" in control because a soul may actually be driving the current behavior based on human motivations accumulated over more than one lifetime.

Controlling vs. Accepting. The need to control our lives and surroundings arises from blind animal fear that something will happen to threaten survival. All animals have a "comfort zone," places and behaviors within which their survival instinct does not feel threatened. The human animal feels the same way. So it attempts to construct its own comfort zone(s) by controlling all the variables around it. Unfortunately, that often includes controlling other people's behavior when their actions are inconsistent with one's own comfort zone parameters.

Because Light Beings feel no fear, we have no need to control what goes on around us. We are free to accept things as they are, secure in the knowledge that a being composed entirely of Energy cannot be harmed. Light Beings also understand they have invested themselves into human forms to experience the richness of events and emotions Earth life has to offer. They make no judgments about experiences, labeling some good and others bad, as humans do, because all experiences are worthwhile and precious to us in our spiritual form. They all present opportunities for evolution back to our Source.

The soul's personality may also be controlling if that is what was learned from the body, parents, and society during this or other lifetimes. The inexperienced soul readily adopts human fear of the unknown, for it comes into this world with complete amnesia about who it is and why it is here. We must wake up to our true nature to access knowledge that will enable us to suppress this fear and need for control.

Although the body feels the fear and is motivated to control its environment to eliminate it, it is the personality of the soul that often translates emotion into complex action. A very inexperienced soul lacking in ability to control its host, or a human being without a soul[30], may simply act on animal impulse. A prime example is violence. Using violence simply to control others seems to be a behavior limited to humans. Although other animals can be very violent, their motive is always survival. Humans, on the other hand, are capable of very complex motivations and express them through various types of violence, especially when they feel they have no way to control their own environment or life.

Some violence is no more than using physical strength to control others, like any other animal would. Such behavior stems from fear of not getting one's own way, which is important in controlling the environment, itself a necessity to alleviate fear of the unknown. Light Being souls who are unaware of their eternal nature may well fuel the fires of fear and violence by adding motivations, stockpiled hurts, and rationalizations. That is why it is so important to wake up to the reality of your Light Being nature. Then you can escape fear and can work to relieve the body's fears in a non-violent way.

Accepting the unknown, accepting fear of the unknown, and moving outside one's own comfort zone is the first step toward shifting from animal to Light Being motivated behavior. To take this step, however, we must retrain our own bodies and souls. The body must be taught that the soul's choices will protect it from harm. The soul must be trained to overcome one or more lifetime(s)' behavior imprinting during childhood so that it can indeed protect its host. The knowledge, love, and courage to undertake these tasks are all *within* by nature—our eternal nature.

Competitive vs. Collaborative. The human animal feels anxiety over its place in a hierarchical world when forced to compete for scarce survival necessities. Cave men, for example, might have had to compete for animal meat in winter months. They found that when the choice was between competing for food or starving, aggression of the alpha male type served their needs best. Survival of the fittest. Natural selection. Both are animal-based evolutionary concepts. And those concepts have been handed down both genetically and socially generation after generation. Genetically, through the *homo sapiens* species; socially, through habit and parents training their children, who train their children, on and on.

The alpha male has the best chance of controlling his environment and therefore minimizing fear of the known and unknown. So male humans compete for that distinction. Anxiety over whether one is an alpha male, or one-up on others, permeates the personalities of some human beings. Where one fits into the hierarchy of animals determines who gets the best job, the most suitable mate, and the best chance of survival. Those concerns have been translated in modern society into competition. Competition for money, sex, and recognition.

Our soul personalities have integrated the concept of competition, which once related only to survival, into the fabric of life in societies where it no longer serves a useful purpose. We have had to create artificial battlefields to perpetuate and justify competitive behavior based on an animal instinct that should have evolved out of humans thousands of years ago. Games and sports offer the most obvious artificial battlefields. The desire for social standing creates another. The lust for competition begins in childhood with competitive sports and the quest for good grades. Parents even compete with each other vicariously through their children's accomplishments. Competition has been used as a motivator in the workplace. Even in social life we compete, men for bragging rights and women for attention. Competition has become the human way of life.

The compelling New York Times best-selling book by Deborah Tannen, Ph.D., entitled *You Just Don't Understand: Women and Men in Conversation*, demonstrates how ingrained competition has become in our world. Dr. Tannen's book both enlightens and entertains the reader with why men and women miscommunicate so often, and gives this insightful description of how men and women view the world, resulting in different approaches to life and thus conversation:

> Having done the research that led to this book, I now see that my husband was simply engaging the world in a way that many men do: as an individual in a hierarchical social order in which he was either one-up or one-down. In this world, conversations are negotiations in which people try to achieve and maintain the upper hand if they can, and protect themselves from others' attempts to put them down and push them around. Life, then, is a contest, a struggle to preserve independence and avoid failure.
>
> I, on the other hand, was approaching the world as many women do: as an individual in a network of connections. In this world, conversations are negotiations for closeness in which people try to seek and give confirmation and support, and to reach consensus. They try to protect themselves from others' attempts to push them away. Life, then, is a community, a struggle to preserve intimacy and avoid isolation. Though there are hierarchies in this world, too, they are hierarchies more of friendship than of power and accomplishment.

Women are also concerned with achieving status and avoiding failure, but these are not the goals they are *focused* on all the time, and they tend to pursue them in the guise of connection. And men are also concerned with achieving involvement and avoiding isolation, but they are not *focused* on these goals, and they tend to pursue them in the guise of opposition.[31]

Dr. Tannen's book is about conversational styles as they are influenced by whether a person sees life as a threatening, competitive struggle for power and success, or as a network of close, supportive connections that ward off isolation and loneliness. But her work is more universal than that.

These two conversational styles mirror the differences between the human body and the Light Being within. The human viewpoint, based largely on animal instinct to compete for survival, could be said to be like that of the male described by Dr. Tannen. The Light Being, on the other hand, would favor the cooperation and emotional closeness attributed to the female view Dr. Tannen describes. Light Beings know that all of us are connected within Source, and that no hierarchy is necessary because all of creation is equal, and all returns to Source as the culmination of evolution.

Many cultures view acting like a woman to be weakness, the psychological equivalent of castration. Yet adopting the female perspective of collaboration and cooperation actually leads us to the far more powerful resources of our Light Being state. We can train ourselves to overcome the stigma associated with what is deemed "female" behavior and adopt this more evolved approach to life. All that is required is a change in perspective.

Status Quo vs. Change. A refusal to learn anything new, resistance to new ideas, and adamant adherence to the status quo are all symptoms of fear of the unknown. Animal fear. Humans fear change because it is, by definition, a foray into the unknown.

Light Beings know that those who rail against change are fighting an impossible battle. It is the very nature of Sourcebeams to return to Source in a changed form. That is the whole point of evolution. And the fastest route to evolution is learning, experiencing, and trying new things and ideas. The more you learn and integrate into your thinking the broader your perspective. Inasmuch as one of the goals of human habitation is to experience all perspectives on every aspect of human life, the faster you do that through learning, the sooner you will achieve reunification with Source.

We can retrain our bodies to reduce fear of the unknown so that we can enjoy new experiences. Psychologists have techniques for doing this. So do support groups. Some resistance to new experiences may be pure addiction to habitual ways of acting. Those habits can be broken with effort and new ones adopted that allow for more spontaneity. That is one of the wonderful things about human nature. Once you adopt a desire to learn and grow, that goal can be integrated into the body's habits through behavior modification.

Self-Centered vs. Whole-Centered. It is human nature to be self-centered, for, after all, an animal's sole purpose is to survive. Every thought and act must be geared toward maximizing survival potential. But humans often carry that to an extreme. American society in particular seems to be dominated by people who give no thought to anything but fulfilling their own needs. We lock ourselves behind doors, iron grids, security systems, and bulletproof glass because so many humans pillage our businesses and homes, like wild animals seeking food. Rudeness and inconsideration pervade our interactions as though we were in life-or-death competition for every morsel of food. The road to business success is over the backs of broken bodies. Generations ago it was common to keep both human and eternal life in mind on a daily basis. But now we have allowed animal self-centeredness to overtake what used to be known as "humanity."

Many other examples of humans' disregard for each other as part of one whole appear in the news everyday. In a society where we uniformly abhor cruelty to domestic animals, we routinely turn a blind eye to people who eat to the point of causing themselves diabetes and heart disease. We think nothing of killing and maiming each other, though we would never tolerate the presence in our society of persons who would maim and kill cats and dogs. How many news stories have you seen about someone who allows fifteen cats to live in their own filth, starving to death, resulting in public outcry that the government must step in to rescue the animals. Yet we allow human beings–whole families, children–to live on the street, or to be imported in boxcars, living in their own filth and squalor during their travels. We have homeless people living under bridges out in the cold and damp. And we support a government that subsidizes the growth and manufacture of tobacco, a product that is nothing but pure poison, which causes lung cancer in many who consume it, and in those who are simply in the vicinity of smokers.

The Light Being instinctively knows that all of creation is One. An awakened soul will remember that everything created resides within Source and is therefore equally deserving of respect and attention. While our primary obligation is our own evolution, once awakened to our Light Being nature we realize that everyone else's evolution is just as important. The old adage of being "thy brother's keeper" is real and true, and creates an obligation to put the best interests of *both* self and others at the forefront.

Some enlightened people, especially women, swing the pendulum too far in the opposite direction from self-centeredness. They neglect their own needs in favor of serving others. That lifestyle is only half on target, for self-sacrifice contradicts our prime directive to treat everyone, including self, equally well.

It is important while seeking awareness that we train ourselves to honor and respect all of creation, all creatures, including each other. Remember we are all one Being and what we do affects the entire fabric of the universe. This truth will come to us as "knowing" once we allow ourselves to access Universal Knowledge. And, as we comprehend the Oneness of creation, we can retrain our actions to reflect the reverence we feel for all of it.

Irresponsible vs. Super-Responsible. Lack of interest in the consequences of one's own behavior is an animal trait, for the animal's only goal is day-to-day survival. Animals accept no responsibility for the consequences of their actions because they are instinctual. Human animals are no different. Refusal to accept responsibility for one's own behavior can range from a global level, such as denial that burning fossil fuels is polluting the atmosphere; to a local level, like denial that violence in the media is destroying its shock value and conditioning younger generations to feel nothing when they see injury and death; to simply denying one's own personal responsibility for another's hurt feelings when you insult them. Blindness to the consequences of human behavior is destroying our planet. Denial of the consequences flowing naturally from mass media exposure is destroying younger generations. Sexually transmitted diseases are epidemic solely because we refuse to take responsibility for our own animal drives and protect others and ourselves.

Light Beings know that everything they do influences everyone else in the continuum of life and Energy that constitutes Source. Acceptance of responsibility for one's own actions is a key feature of Light Being life. Souls become keenly aware of the consequences of their own behavior during their after death life reviews, when they not only see and hear everything they have done, but also feel it from the perspective of all those on the receiving end. Nothing is more traumatic than actually experiencing the consequences of our own unloving behavior while standing in another's shoes, so to speak. While in the body, we are stewing in our own emotions and often cannot get beyond them to appreciate the fact that everything we do, and even feel, affects those around us. But those effects are brought home to us during our life reviews so that we can fully understand not only the unity of Source's creations, but also how our experiences ripple through the fabric of that Oneness.

Make it your goal to move toward taking more responsibility for the consequences of your own actions, even the unforeseen ones. Drop the phrase, "that's his problem," from your vocabulary and you will be edging closer to your Light Being nature. We are our brothers' keepers, in the sense that we are each responsible for the effects of our thoughts, words, deeds, and emotions upon those around us.

Disinterested vs. Curious. Human animal laziness can take the form of anything from living a life comprised of nothing more than eating, sleeping, eliminating, and procreating; to simple neglect of personal and business matters. This type of disinterest in life often springs from fear of the unknown combined with a desire to maintain the status quo. It can also be a reflection of deep and lasting pain accumulated from past experiences. One may easily lose interest in life if living is associated with hurting.

A Being of Light, on the other hand, is motivated to experience everything it can in the human lifetime allotted. Curiosity is our natural inclination.

The combined body/soul being may exhibit both tendencies, enthusiastically engaging in activities of interest, especially playful ones, and entirely ignoring disfavored tasks. The purpose of human life, clearly, is to enjoy it. But try to find joy in more areas of life. Stretch. Grow. Try something new just to be able to say you did. And find something of interest in everything you do, even if it is just enjoying the soothing monotony of cleaning the house or doing dishes.

Judgmental vs. Compassionate. Humans *judge* everything to be good or bad according to survival, religious, or communal standards. Our bodies do this naturally because it is part of survival instinct to be critical of our environment and everything moving within it. We are also taught as children to judge everything when we listen to our parents pronounce their opinions on all they observe. Our parents teach us to judge each other when they say, "That's a bad neighborhood," and "They're not like us," and even the all too necessary, "Beware of strangers." Our societies are built and run on judgments. We choose this house and that school based on our assessments of their benefits versus those of another house and school. Our job choices reflect judgments about our own skills as well as what an employer has to offer us. Our elected officials try to influence our votes with commercials about their judgments on one topic after another, whether it is pro-life vs. pro-choice, or closed borders vs. openness to immigrants. The very freedom upon which most countries are founded rests upon a foundation of judgment. We are free to choose from among options offered as we judge appropriate.

Light Beings do not pass judgment because they understand that everything is always as it should be. It does not matter what we choose because all choices result in experiences that help us grow and evolve. Perhaps the most difficult aspect of Light Being nature to adapt to human life is abandoning the habit of being judgmental. Chapter 15 is devoted to this topic.

Childish vs. Emotionally Mature. The life of a physical being is destined to be self-limiting to those behaviors necessary to create and continue life until it is lost through nature's relentless cycle. It does not take much emotional maturity to sleep, eat, drink, eliminate, collect survival and nesting materials, play, and procreate. While this describes the very rudimentary life of what we would call a lower animal life form, it is not far off target for humans as well. The greater convolutions and complexity of the human brain generate far more sophisticated methods of achieving animal goals, for sure, but they remain animal goals.

For example, the most futuristic piece of equipment for seeing inside the human brain to more precisely remove tumors and identify disease still serves only the animal survival instinct. Whole industries devoted to complex microchips and nanobots ultimately do nothing more than produce work that pays money used to secure survival and nesting materials. The most sophisticated chess and other intellectual games are still play. And no matter how you dress it with ritual, like marriage contracts and religious sacraments, mating is still just propagation of the species. So life as a human does not actually require much emotional development or insight.

Emotional maturity, and even placing value on emotional development, is a Light Being characteristic. The progression of understanding, through experience, insight, enlightenment, and ultimately "knowing" via immersion into Universal Knowledge, is a hallmark of higher evolutionary states—the types of evolution available only to higher life forms like Light Beings. And, while ninety-nine percent of such emotional development may be automatically suppressed upon entering human form, Light Being souls can access it for current use through attention and intention. They appear to "grow up" as they do so. To mature. It is the soul half of the combined being that becomes what we would like to expect an adult to be. The human personality remains childlike in comparison. Psychologists may even refer to it as the "inner child" without realizing they are describing the human part of our duality.

It should not be our goal to eradicate the human's childlike personality as we evolve. Rather, we must heal it, and then foster development of childlike interest and innocence within our soul personalities. The healing will result in release of personality traits formed by fear, anger, guilt, and pain. Chapter 14 discusses this in more detail.

Ego-Driven vs. Altruistic. Many writers have defined the term "ego" to mean many things. Its use here means a tendency to puff oneself up, to make oneself look more important or desirable than he/she might otherwise be, self-aggrandizement, self-adulation. Ego-driven behavior would then be any action taken for the purpose of making one appear grander. Some common examples are boasting, name-dropping, carrying on a monologue about one's own accomplishments, wearing makeup, dying one's hair, and plastic surgery. Some of these are offensive to others, like boasting, while cosmetic enhancements are found acceptable by most.

Light Being nature, on the other hand, is instinctively to do what is best for the whole collective, because we know for certain that what is done to one of us is done to all of us, and to our Source. People who put others' needs and desires ahead of their own may be perceived to be altruistic, but they are in fact self-sacrificing. True Light Being nature treats all beings equally with no intention to sacrifice oneself, for that can be just as damaging as being self-centered. A person acting from Light Being nature will try to devise a solution or action that benefits all equally, including oneself.

There are many more motivations influencing behavior besides the few outlined here. The whole panoply of a person's learned behavior arises from combinations of many of these motives, both human and soul based in origin. And, because we carry over motivations from other lives, many of which are also fear, self-centered, or survival based, the complexity of human behavior cannot be overestimated.

The purpose of understanding what motivates your behavior, and whether it is animal or Light Being in nature, is to increase your choices and further your evolution. Examine your own behavior to see whether you are acting out of survival motivation in situations that are not truly life threatening. Is it really a threat to your body's survival to learn about other religions or cultures? It may be outside your animal comfort zone but it certainly will not kill your body. Is your body going to die if your spouse wants to do something out of the normal routine? Do you really have to control your boyfriend's behavior around your parents because your survival is at stake? Is getting that promotion going to save your life? We often behave as though these were all life-and-death situations.

Why do we act this way? Out of fear. Out of fear, humans have chosen to emulate their animal kingdom companions rather than strive to elevate themselves to higher levels of existence. As a culture, we Americans have reduced ourselves to the lowest common denominator, i.e., survival behaviors.

You can *choose* not to act out animal emotions. You can *choose* to live more aligned with your own true Light Being nature. You can *choose* to evolve more quickly, and, in the process, increase the peace, joy, and unconditional love in your life. Now is a particularly good time in Earth's history to take a more active role in your own evolution, for a healthy dose of Light Being nature will certainly ease the trauma of the upcoming transition between epochs.

Go through the list of human animal and Light Being traits outlined here and see which motivations are at work in your own life. Examine your own behaviors one by one to see if they could possibly fit within one or more of the animal characteristics above. Then ask yourself what your true motivation is—not the surface justification you give yourself now, but the motivation that is really at work down deep inside.

Some religious traditions teach us we should be holy, or act in a holy manner, and they like to define what that means. Some think we should always follow what our souls tell us to do. I believe our job is to act "wholly," meaning a single vibration between body and soul. Body and soul acting in concert. When our vibrations line up, our body and soul sing in harmony. That happens only when we have evolved enough to treat others and ourselves with unconditional love.

The bottom line is: we are not here to allow our unevolved or unhealed souls to control our bodies, to take over living and make all the decisions. Nor should we allow our bodies to lead us around by their noses. We are here to reduce the conflict between humans and us, to harmonize the vibration and grant both beings peace. Harmony will come from re-evaluating our own human and soul personalities and healing those aspects that not only cause us pain, but also impact on everyone else in the commonality of which we are part.

Understanding the basic natures and motivations of the two beings within our duality gives us a foundation for making changes. But it is not alone sufficient. We must accept and even love not only our own personalities, and those of our host bodies, but also the differences between them. Those differences are what draw us to humans, who provide the richness and reward of a physical life experience. The love that is required for this task is unconditional love, a word used often in our society but rarely understood. Let us understand now the differences between the various types of human love and true unconditional love.

12

✳ What Is and Isn't Unconditional Love

We are born into this world full of unconditional love.

Then our parents train it out of us. They do it with the best of intentions. Parents are charged with the duty of preparing their children to live in a world they and others have manifested. An unfriendly world. A dangerous society. Human fear pushes unconditional love into the background. The human animal personality begins its triumph over the soul inside, resulting in our fear-based society, which pushes unconditional love aside. The vicious circle is formed: we learn that love is inextricably bound up with fear, a tragedy of epic proportions.

Much of what our parents taught us about love is backwards. Oh, what they conveyed with their words might have been true enough. They told us that they loved us more than anything. Yet the concept of love we grew up with was still backwards, for, as we all know, actions speak louder than words. Our parents' actions taught us the human version of love. The version based on fear. The type of love that manifests as possessiveness, jealousy, control, and neediness.

It is important to unlearn our fear-based definition of love and replace it with a Light Being's perspective before launching on our evolutionary voyage. Light Beings do not fear. Nor do we ever lose love, for it is our innate character to enjoy unconditional love for all eternity. But we have amnesia about unconditional love and so adopt the types of love we see in this world. These models must be unlearned for they hold us back from the love we need to evolve.

Earning Love. Through our parents' efforts to train us how to behave in society we learned love has to be earned. Gone is the unconditional love of Light Being existence, to be replaced with the belief that we are lovable only when our behavior is acceptable to our parents. One example from my own childhood comes to mind: when our mother would take my sisters and me to visit her friends, she would tell us we had to be good. Her definition of "good" included sitting still and saying no when offered a cookie, even though we really wanted that cookie. If we sat like statutes while she visited with her friend, Mom would tell us on the way home how good we were and how much she loved us. The mental connection was formed in our little hearts. Mom's perfectly rightful attempt to make us behave in other people's homes was unintentionally teaching us that she loved us only when we comply—the very definition of conditional love. A more appropriate reward for good behavior in this context would have been the cookie.

When we teach children that love is associated with good behavior, they learn love and fear go hand-in-hand. Fear of losing a parent's love, their protection, and nurturing, for misbehavior that is bound to happen is a crushing weapon. Fear that we are not acceptable for who we really are destroys us, as does fear that there are parts of us that make us unlovable. This fear continues to dominate our human experience making us selfish with our love. Leading us to force others to earn it.

Often we choose friends and lovers not for their soul personality, but for what they do for us. We pick friends who give us free products or professional advice, or because they have a boat or vacation cabin, or because they like to go to football games. If you would no longer be interested in being friends with someone if they stopped giving free goods or services, or sold their boat or cabin, or stopped going to football games, you have made your friends "earn" your love.

So many souls believe the backwards notion that love must be earned that the institution of marriage is founded on this false premise. Men and women do their best to earn marriage by saying and doing exactly what they believe the other wants. Women try to earn marriage with sex, and expect men to reciprocate by fathering children and providing whatever lifestyle women seek. Men try to earn it with money and success, and expect women to reciprocate with sex and providing the types of home life men seek. Then, after wedding vows are exchanged, both parties start taking each other for granted and revert to their normal pre-dating behavior. This change in the relationship causes much heartache, with each party feeling the other no longer loves and appreciates him/her, simply because both have stopped trying to *earn* the other's love.

Unconditional love literally means love that is not contingent upon our behaving as the other wishes. It is love of *who we are,* not what we do. There are no strings attached.

> Unconditional love does not seek to own, or change. It does not seek to possess, or judge, or uphold expectations of any kind (hence it is called **un**conditional). It asks that we love people, all people, all stemming from the same Source.[32]

As I discovered during the life review portion of my life after death, unconditional love includes unconditional acceptance despite behavior. Because it is their nature, the Light Being friends I met totally loved me notwithstanding what I judged to be my rather miserable attempt to live a soul-directed life on Earth. Unconditional love is our inborn nature too. We can and do unconditionally love our children, and each other, despite behaviors we will not tolerate. We need to make that clearer in our relationships. Divorce the concept of "earning" from the concept of love.

Deal with behavior problems separately from expressions of love. Tell your child or loved one that you love *him/her* as a person no matter what he/she does. And *mean* it. Then, when a behavior issue arises, assure your loved one that your love for him/her has not changed, and will not change, no matter how the behavior issue is resolved. Humans/souls believe their behaviors are a reflection of who they are, and that criticism of behavior constitutes a rejection of them as beings. We have to teach our loved ones that a behavior is not who they *are* as a person; it is only a choice, even if it has now become habit, and a new behavior choice can be made. Make it clear that the specified behavior, not the person, is unacceptable under the circumstances, and that some resolution of the issue has to be reached to keep peace.

The resolution may require new choices by both parties. For example, if a child will only play games with others when he is allowed to win, one resolution would be for the child to learn how to let others win, and for the parents to learn to stop conditioning the child to believe winning is more important than the joy of playing. The latter may require the parents to choose not to praise their child for winning, which will feel wrong to them because it is human nature to be competitive. Instead, try following Light Being nature and praise the child for having a fun relationship with his friends.

In a marriage example, if one spouse decides he wants multiple sex partners and the other feels betrayed by that choice, one resolution might be to end the marriage. The parties can still love each other, yet not be willing to share a lifestyle that meets the needs of only one of them. Even a divorce can be navigated without severe emotional damage if that is the resolution agreed upon by both parties out of unconditional love for each other.

Another resolution might be negotiated if both parties are willing to set aside their lifelong training in how *not* to love, and diligently apply themselves to finding a solution that honors both parties' needs and desires while maintaining unconditional love for the other.

Love and Manipulation. Childhood training also teaches us to equate love with control. How often have we heard, in various forms, "If you loved me, you would do what I say"? We watch our parents and family members manipulate each other this way and adopt that as our model for love. You cannot control another's life in an attempt to assure yourself of their love. Control is about fear. Fear that you will lose love. Fear that you will be alone. Animal fear.

Real love is open and honest. Unconfining. Uncontrolled and uncontrollable. If you feel a need to manipulate someone to get them to do what you want, you do not love *them*, you love what they are going to do for you, or what you think they are going to do for you, or what you think you can get them to do for you. You are back to making someone earn your love.

You have to *attract* loved ones every minute of every hour of every day. Be so attractive in personality that your loved ones crave being around you. Broadcast enough unconditional love to intoxicate all you encounter. Give love away freely. Do not make others earn it by manipulating their emotions to control their behavior.

Love and Possessiveness. Possessiveness has no place in love. We cannot possess another in any form. In our natural state as Light Beings we do have the ability to literally merge into those we love. But that is not possession, for it honors the worth and equality of the other. As Light Beings we know that nothing can be truly possessed, least of all another representative of Source's self-awareness. Everything is connected in one enormous web of Source Energy field/being. Nothing is ever cut out and allocated solely to one person. It is only the illusion of separateness the amnesiac soul endures that allows us to think we possess anything, including our own individuality.

Perhaps we vaguely remember the intimacy of being merged with Source before we were Earth-bound, for we all intuitively seek completion through relationships with others. But the human experience is about separateness. Individuality. We are here precisely to experience that feeling. And it imposes an artificial disconnection from the sensation that we are all One that cannot be rectified by attempts to force another to love us.

Possessiveness is fear-based. Human fear. It is about control and fear of losing. More than that, it signifies a deeply rooted belief that the other, whoever that may be, is not as valuable as I am. A belief that the other can be owned and controlled like material goods. A belief that I have the *right* to command the other's attention and affections for myself because I want them. It is self-centeredness—another animal trait. Nothing is more indicative of a lack of love for who the person *is* than possessiveness, for it completely negates acknowledgement of the other's existence as a self-aware being.

Unconditional love by definition can exist only between and among equals. It is love given to someone who is accepted as is. Love is not conditioned upon the beloved taking a subservient position, a lower status, for that kind of relationship is designed to artificially flatter the human ego of the person in the higher position or status. An unequal relationship between adults is servitude, not love. The generations upon generations of human history of women being subjugated to male dominance is animal behavior based on the alpha-male model. The fact that such a model is not extinct is a sad testament to how little we have evolved the human species since entering primitive man.

Love and Neediness. Those of us who have physical infirmities, or who are challenged financially or emotionally, present opportunities for another type of emotion disguised as love to take hold. Neediness and gratitude for having those needs fulfilled can masquerade as love if we are not careful. Many marriages are based more on the wife's and children's need for financial and lifestyle support than on true appreciation and reverence for who the husband is as a person. Many other marriages remain intact out of sheer gratitude for the spouse's contributions to the union, whatever they may be. Interdependence is an admirable quality in a pair-bonding. But an unbalanced mating, where one spouse is being used for his/her role in fulfilling every day needs without being given unconditional love and respect, is not honorable. Both parties must learn to love and respect each other's spiritual self before true love will enter the relationship.

Similarly, parent-child relationships must recognize their respective souls' equality while preserving the teacher-student relationship of the age difference. The child's body must be trained and his/her soul reared to live in existing society. But the existence of these parental duties does not reduce the child's equality as a being. Children should be treated with unconditional love, recognizing their needs occasioned by age and immaturity, but not subjugated as though they are worth less than adults. The inclination to treat the young and old as burdens to the herd because of their infirmities as compared to the full strength adult is animal behavior. It is not love.

Love and Relationships. If unconditional love is love of who we are, not what we do, then how are we to choose whom to love? Easy. You do *not* have to choose. That is the meaning of unconditional. There are no conditions under which you must choose to love one person instead of another. All are lovable. Equally. That is the bliss of Source love. Unconditional love means you do not love only people who have skin the same color as yours. You do not love only those who follow the same religion you do. You do not love only your family because you share DNA with them. You do not love only Americans because you live in

America. Unconditional love is one-size-fits-all. It means loving the human animal just because it is Source Energy. Loving the soul within just because it is Source awareness. Loving everything in creation simply because, like you, it is a manifestation of Source.

Do not confuse love with choice. Love is for all. Choice of relationship may be reserved for the few. You choose to bring a child into human life, and you feel parental love arising out of that choice. You choose whether someone you meet, or work with, or live near, will be a friend and feel friendship love in that relationship. You choose your spouse to feel the love of pair-bonding inherent in animal mating. These are all choices of relationships, and they all have loving feelings that accompany them, but they should not be choices of whom to love to the exclusion of all others.

Humans have love and choice so jumbled up together that they have attached a hierarchy to love based on the degree of physical intimacy of the relationship. Parent-child love is the highest in the hierarchy for it is truly the most intimate, especially for women. Then comes love of family, with bloodline intimacy. Then spousal love with its sexual intimacy. Friendship is usually last because it generally has no physical intimacy. Do you see how this system is animal based? Love based on biology is the result of human animal survival instincts. The relationship, and therefore love, that perpetuates the species is given a higher priority.

This is all so backwards! The emotion of love comes from the soul, from our Light Being nature, not the body. All human forms of love are watered-down versions of our true nature of unconditional love. The predomination of human animal personality in our world has influenced our experience of love, and caused us to believe that we should love only those with whom we have an animal connection. That is instinct! Not love. We need to unhook our idea of love from choice of relationship in order to see it for what it really is.

Love is not something you find; it is something you *are*. You do not *find* someone to love. Love is *shared*, meaning you have to first feel it yourself, as part of your nature. You may *find* another with whom you *choose* to have a relationship of one type or another. But that is a lifestyle choice, not a trigger for the emotion of love. The current model we have of holding all our love inside until we find someone whom we believe has earned it is a fear-based endeavor. It is the animal model of hoarding food for winter; we hoard love until we can use it to buy certain behaviors from others. It is our true Light Being nature to be full of love all the time. Love does not have to be hoarded. In fact, the more we give it away the more we feel it, for we are opening ourselves up to the universal flow of love from Source.

Trust is the antidote to fear in relationships and opens us up to having more of them, to choosing more emotionally intimate relationships. We need to trust that our loved one will not harm us before we can let down our guard and love them. We have to trust that the other will not judge us, will not reject us, once we show our true selves. In short, we require unconditional love from others before we deign to love them back. Perhaps it is time to extend unconditional love to others first, and allow that love to attract others who are evolved enough to share it.

Love and Mating. Rather than asking how we should choose whom to love, we should be asking ourselves, "how can we keep fear out of the process of choosing a mate?"

The role models we have chosen for men and women in today's society have been outdated for generations. Yet they persist out of fear and habit. Humans are so resistant to change that progress takes hundreds, if not thousands, of years. That resistance is born of fear–fear that any minor change in status quo will destroy humans' control over their lives and all that is in them. In truth, humans do not control their lives or the world around them. Souls do. The Light Beings within are the ones with the ability to manifest reality in the form of matter, not the human body. Yet, we ignore our own natural abilities and permit human fear to dictate our relationships. That fear is so ancient, and so bound up with survival, that it has retarded the human species from evolving. Nowhere is that more evident than in "loving" relationships between males and females.

Mating is strictly a human animal instinct. So it makes sense from an animal's perspective that mates be selected based solely on animal attraction and behaviors. But humans/souls are not just animals. Most of the combined being's personality is in the soul, not the body. A tradition of ignoring that iceberg and focusing on the tip has resulted in more than half of all marriages and long-term relationships imitating the *Titanic*. We must stop picking mates like animals and start forming pair-bonds based upon compatibility of the souls within if we want to experience unconditional love in that context.

A loving relationship between two people should be a safe haven. It is the closest we can get to the sensation of merger with Source while in the body. It should be an opportunity for two souls to share all they are with each other, as is done when two Light Beings merge. That kind of intimacy requires total trust—the kind of trust that comes only from an intimate knowledge and awareness of each other's true nature. Our marriages and other pair-bonds would be stronger and last longer if the choice to enter into that type of relationship were based on the personality and character of the soul rather than the appearance of the body.

Getting to know another soul intimately requires time and honesty. It takes a considerable amount of time for two people to explore each other's thoughts, beliefs, fears, hopes, preferences, and prejudices through both conversation, and observation in diverse situations. It requires a considerable amount of honesty. Informed choices cannot be made on the basis of puffery or self-delusion. So one must know himself or herself intimately before he/she can experience an honest relationship with another.

We must start any relationship with that same unconditional love for the other person that we hold for all of creation. The other does not have to earn love. He/she does not have to behave in any particular way to earn our respect, for we respect all of Source's creations. It is not our job to judge the other, only to decide whether he/she is a person with whom we wish to have a pair-bonding relationship. Then we must take the time and put forth the effort to get to know the other's human and soul personalities through communication and observation.

Although animal attraction may have sparked our initial interest, following through with that by having sex before we truly know the other will only deluge us with old fear-based models of love because we have shifted the foundation of the relationship to the animal model. This does not mean that sex is immoral or bad in any way. My beyond-death experience convinced me that sex is a beautiful, healthy, normal human animal function that we should enjoy without guilt. However, if the goal of the moment is to determine whether a particular person is a potential pair-bonding mate, it is important to reduce the temptation to slide back into an old animal-based model of love. Sexual activity is the most intimate sharing of beings that souls can know in the flesh. And that intimacy riddles the situation with fear of rejection, loss, and inadequacy. Fear of looking foolish to others or ourselves. Fear of failure at the relationship. All this fear will make it impossible to conduct the relationship at the level of unconditional love. Why jinx the budding romance with the burden of having to dig out of a hole of fear-based love before it can evolve to one more typical of Light Being nature?

Similarly, acting as though we are already pair-bonded by living together before making a permanent commitment may bring into play old views of love bound up with fear, including neediness, possessiveness, and forcing the other to earn our love through behaviors acceptable to us. This is because an entire lifestyle is at risk. It is human animal nature to use all its wiles to secure food, shelter, and other living necessities. So it is natural for the human animal to want to control his/her mate's contribution to their shared lifestyle—part of its survival instinct. With so much at stake on an animal instinct level it is exceedingly difficult to relax and get to know the potential mate on a soul level. It is much easier to maintain unconditional love, and then make the pair-bonding decision on the basis of true knowledge and understanding of and compassion for the other, if fear-based models of mating are avoided.

Love and Pain. Both body and soul associate the human experience of love with pain. Pain of loss. Grieving the death of a loved one. Disappointment that a relationship did not last. Sympathy pains for an injured offspring. The pain of love springs from the well of caring what happens to our loved ones and ourselves. Caring whether we could have changed the outcome had we done something differently. It is human nature to care about the events of this world and their impact on our emotions.

The pain of loving is one of the many reasons Light Beings choose to assume human life, for it is an aspect of life more informative, and therefore growth-oriented, than any other. Pain tells us we are alive in a way only physical matter can be. It tells us we are tender. That our emotions are healthy and our sensitivities intact. Emotional pain grabs our attention and forces us to examine our behavior choices, giving us a mini-preview of our ultimate life review. It reminds us that we are capable of love despite our fears..

The pain of human love stayed with me during the early phases of my transition in the Light. Throughout my life review I suffered the pain of loss, disappointment, and my own condemnation for my behavior. Yet the pain was not at all associated with how others had treated *me*, but rather how I had treated them. I felt *their* pain. All the pain I could have alleviated had I acted from unconditional love, instead of fear and self-interest.

It was not until I completed the transition and began living life as a Light Being, perusing the Universal Knowledge database, that the pain of human love dissipated. Unconditional love in the Light carries no pain burden for we no longer care about human events. For example, while the history of Earth events played out before my eyes I no longer cared what happened to my loved ones who were still in the flesh. It was not that I stopped loving them, for my love had been elevated to loftier heights than I could have imagined. But fear had been taken out of the equation. I knew for a certainty that no real harm could befall my loved ones because Light Being souls cannot be mortally harmed. Thus, I discovered that "caring" what happens to loved ones is actually fear-driven.

Humans fear the sensation and consequences of pain, and so care when it rears its ugly head. We care about our sons and daughters being hurt in their mating relationships because we fear how they will handle the pain. Will they descend into the chasm of depression? Drink their way into oblivion? Become angry and bitter? We fear the consequences of our own losses and how they will change our personalities. Will we survive the loss? Of course we will, for the human body adapts to most anything, but emotional pain is as real in its debilitating potential as physical pain. We fear life will never be enjoyable again, and that our love of life will not survive the loss.

Once again we see that human animal fear controls how we love—the "good," as well as the "bad," aspects. Fear generates both caring and control, two common features of human love.

In soul form our habit may be to view the world, and love, from the perspective of looking from inside our host bodies outward. We fear loving because of its consequences. We manipulate, make others earn our love, and act possessive of loved ones because we project our inner fear outward through our behavior choices.

Allowing knowledge of our Light Being nature to broaden our perspective to a universal level will help us grow to love the universe and everyone in it without fear. We will begin to understand that we are all here to evolve, grow at our own paces, and learn from our own choices. When someone interferes with the experiences we choose (perhaps chose even before we were born), though they do it with loving intentions, it interferes with our evolution. And because all of creation is linked, the ripple effect of fear-based love is crippling our world.

All of our old, habitual, fear-based concepts of love have to be discarded in favor of a new beginning. We can experience it just by letting go of fear. We feel free to love the beauty of blossoming wild flowers, raspberry sunsets, and hushed snow blankets because we do not fear they will hurt us. In the same way, we can be free to truly love Source when we relinquish the idea that it will punish us for misbehavior. And we will be free to unconditionally love each other when we learn that love is a constant in our nature, that it does not have to be earned, and that it is not contingent upon the type of relationship we have with each other.

13

Reeducation

Incorporating behaviors based on our Light Being nature, indeed even changing our beliefs, requires effort. We have to break one habit and train ourselves to another. That is how the human animal learns, and the structure within which our souls must operate while in human form. We now have the tools—attention and intention—to focus on the goal. And we have the knowledge: a deeper understanding of both human and Light Being nature, and the discernment to know which being is motivating our behavior at a given time. We also have a better understanding of love, not only for ourselves as dual beings but also for those with whom we interact. Now it is time to apply those tools to recasting our beliefs and retraining our behaviors.

Self-Training. Once you have convinced yourself that you want to change, you will have to retrain your thoughts, words, and deeds to substitute new attitudes or actions for old ones. One method that has worked for me follows.

I once had a terrible habit of saying anything that popped into my head, including some very unkind and hurtful things. Some were disguised in the form of humor, but were still biting. After my beyond-death experience I tried harder to break this habit.

I started by paying more attention to what I was saying. I *listened* to myself. At first I did not *hear* what I said, or at least realize its hurtful content, until days or weeks after the fact. I resolved to try to be more aware of how my comments affected others. Eventually I started realizing something I said was hurtful within days of saying it, instead of weeks. Then, with renewed attention and intention, I shortened the time lag to hours instead of days. Finally, with perseverance, I was able to recognize my insults right after they flew out of my mouth.

Hearing some of what I said made me ashamed of myself. So I apologized sincerely to the person to whom I said it. At first that apology came weeks after the fact, then days, then hours, then immediately after I made the hurtful remark, as I built up the courage to confess my hurtful behavior and take responsibility for it.

I reasoned that, now that I was "catching" my bad habit right after I engaged in it, I should be able to catch those nasty words before I said them. At first I did not notice an insult was escaping until near the end. Then over time I would catch them half way through. Finally, after months and months of practice, I recognized an insult in formation before it flew through my teeth and I was able to bite down on it.

I resolved next to catch the snide remarks as they were forming in my mind. At first they seemed to just *be* there instantly. All I could do was just keep them there, in my mind but not let them out of my mouth. For years I walked around with a continuous monologue of wisecracks, snide remarks, and snippy comments going on in my head at the same time I was trying to carry on a respectful conversation. Many times I had to apologize to someone for laughing inappropriately or having a look on my face completely out of line with what they were saying, explaining that I was reacting to the laugh track in my head, and not what they were telling me. Eventually the hurtful thoughts stopped. But not entirely—for I still have human nature, which can be cruel, as part of my duality.

This self-training method has helped me break a lot of old habits and to replace some of them with behaviors more in line with who I really am. The same or other methods might work for you too. The prominent feature of whatever self-training method you adopt must be self-awareness, for we cannot change what we do not know exists.

Beyond individual training, we need societal reeducation.

A New Educational System. New mothers are taught to stimulate their babies' minds by talking to them, reading to them, playing music, and exposing them to colors, sights, and sounds. Scientific wisdom says that new stimuli help the brain to grow, to develop. At the same time, our intelligence as souls is being stimulated so that it can be accessed.

In America, we continue this mental stimulation for twelve to sixteen years, depending upon whether one goes to college. Then it stops, as though our brains and souls have exhausted their capacities for stimulation and learning. But we have not exhausted our growth potential at the ripe old age of eighteen, twenty-two, or twenty-five. As we gain in life experiences we also gain in creative potential, for the more we experience, the more platforms we have from which to launch our creativity. We must continue to activate ourselves and our bodies with new ideas, thoughts, and stimuli for an entire lifetime. The more we do so, the more we will call upon our innate creative ability and tap our inexhaustible supply of curiosity. And, the more Light Being nature we bring into this human life, the more energy, joy, love, and evolution we will gain.

The process of education, from cradle to grave, should revolve around love. Love of learning. Love showered on the student in the form of praise and constructive guidance. The kind of love that reflects joy in the student's growth and evolution. It is our very nature to love to learn, for the curiosity of our Source quickens deep within us.

Punishment for failure to learn, either in an arbitrary time frame or to the arbitrary standards set by parents or teachers, crushes that curiosity. Mangles that love. Criticism, low grades, ridicule, and punishment all tap into animal nature. These tools are effective, yes, because human animal nature is strong and keen. Fear is a powerful motivator. So is anger. Yet, strong as human nature may be, that strength is infinitesimal compared to the strength of the universe, the strength of Source, the strength of love right inside that toughened outer physical casing. We can design learning tools that play to our inner strength instead of animal survival instincts.

A new educational paradigm is needed for the Third Epoch. An educational framework that rewards the student for each increment in learning must replace the old system of competing for grades and honors. Competition is an animal life model. Cooperation and collaboration in learning fosters not only the desired behavior— education—but also sparks the love and curiosity that will support lifetime growth.

America's formal education system is ripe for a complete overhaul, and transitioning to the Third Epoch is a perfect time to do it. The current practice of making children learn, and even memorize, factoids of little relevance to their everyday lives started during a time in history when it was possible for one person to learn a little about just about every topic known to humankind. But as humans have evolved, more and more information has been accessed from Universal Knowledge, and the body of facts currently available to us far outstrips what one person can know, or even want to know. There are whole topics—each a discrete body of knowledge—that exceed what one person can learn in a lifetime. So it makes no sense to continue an education system based on a weak attempt to learn facts and skills useful hundreds of years ago, but no longer.

A better education system from the soul's standpoint would be to expose children to the myriad subjects and topics of formal education, along with the tools to find more, and teach them what duality of beings means.

Showing children a sample of a multitude of interesting topics, instead of a few in depth, not only informs them about what is out there to learn but it can spark an interest that can lead to a vocation. Students can then be taught how to research further any subject or field of knowledge that interests them. Research and self-teaching skills would be an integral part of the curriculum I propose.

In addition, formal education should raise children's awareness levels about the duality of their natures. While I understand that the U.S. Constitution requires separation of church and state, public education can still teach the duality of the human/soul because it is a universal phenomenon, unrelated to any Earthly religion. In the schools I envision, children would be taught how to meditate and other means of accessing their own Light Being nature and Universal Knowledge. They would be taught how to relate to one another with unconditional love and all that it means. The traditions of teaching competition for grades and sports acclaim would be abandoned.

Children would learn basic living skills, ranging from how to read, write and do any necessary math; to how to be a friend, find a mate, and parent children. Everything that a young dual being would need could be taught through formal education, if only we were open to change on this scale.

Adults may believe they are too old to learn, but that is a human myth. Many professions have continuing education requirements, attesting to the falsity of the adage that an old dog cannot learn new tricks. Similar types of seminars and educational retreats can be structured to reeducate adults in the "knowing" set forth in Part I. Reading lists can be compiled and disseminated to inform adults of the wealth of information about life and death already available. Study groups have been formed to discuss *A Course in Miracles* and other metaphysical works, and more can be organized. More importantly, adults must be instructed in the ways of accessing their own Light Being Energy in order to open themselves to Universal Knowledge unique and special to their own current lives.

Most of us will need some type of formal education in the "knowings" outlined in Part I, in how to develop awareness, and in how to incorporate more of our true spiritual nature into our lives.

Advertising and Mass Media. Lastly, we must change our mass media messages to reflect Universal Knowledge concepts instead of ancient human ways of thinking, in order to have the greatest impact on the largest number of people. An entire multi-billion dollar industry—advertising—is founded upon the fact that humans are herd animals. Advertisers know that all they have to do to generate sales is present some high-profile person endorsing their product and the herd will follow. And, once the first purchase is made, advertising relies upon the fact that humans, like all animals, act mostly out of habit, and will continue buying that product until distracted from it by another idol promoting something else. So advertising and mass media could be used to re-educate, as well as reinforce other forms of retraining, by redirecting ads from solely generating a profit to informing a society about how all can be at peace and have contentment.

Watching evening TV discloses how commercials can be aimed at Light Being nature rather than human nature. For example, an Ortho Weed-B-Gone commercial shows two men charging down their driveways to a cowboy-like competitive background soundtrack to blast weeds sprouting from cracks in the concrete with weed killer. The Ortho product, of course, wins the competition. That commercial appeals to the human animal trait of competition—the alpha male instinct to win the survival challenge. It also plays on the human fear that one is not manly and virile if he cannot win the competition. Target, on the other hand, has a commercial that appeals to the Light Being nature of curiosity and creativity. It shows many different products morphing into each other to the tune of a ditty, "Say something new about you." See how easy it is to adapt mass media to promote Light Being viewpoints and values and still sell products?

All TV and radio stations are required by law to include public service announcements in their broadcasting. One station uses TV and movie stars to mouth sound bytes that promote education and denounce drugs and smoking. Broad scale reeducation about the truth of our existence could be promoted in the same manner.

One brave TV news anchorman in Cleveland, Ohio has taken a step toward the Third Epoch's enlightened society by broadcasting weekly evening news segments on spirituality. Bringing that kind of awareness to the general public is a truly evolved, loving peek into what mankind has in store in the future. More than that, it is a courageous attempt to reeducate all of us to our spiritual nature. More is needed. On a grander scale.

14

Self-Healing

One of the most devastating tragedies we can suffer is the serious illness of our human host. Although as souls we know the body's evolutionary path is to grow infirm and ultimately die, both body and soul grieve this eventuality when illness calls longevity into question. The body knows innately that it will cease to exist—the ultimate defeat of its survival instinct. We know we will lose a lifelong friend and companion, a being whose every moment of existence has been inextricably bound to our own experience of this lifetime.

Emotional trauma can be as debilitating as loss of life. We assume logically that emotions should be short-lived. An event surfaces, anger is expressed, and then the incident is forgotten. We believe we can "blow off" emotional traumas. Push through them. Get over them. Stuff them. Then how does the body become affected by emotional baggage the soul has carried over from previous lives? Emotional wounds imbedded in our eternal personalities and stored physically in the body can and must be healed.

The combined fear and grief of physical or emotional injury can be crushing and add further devastation to the body. But it need not be that way. Both body and soul have innate healing powers. To heal yourself, you must believe you can. Our bodies/souls can self-heal through the mechanism of manifesting.

Light Beings have the natural ability to manifest what humans perceive as reality, including the reality of the physical status of their bodies. Now, clearly a Light Being cannot defy human nature's evolutionary path, which culminates in its return to the chemical composition of earthly elements. All of creation is bound by the laws of nature of its type of physical matter—its Source-given vibration as an energy pattern. But a Being of Light can manifest well-being for its host within the context of the soul's intended course of learning.

In addition, our bodies are designed to automatically seek homeostasis, meaning a state of balance. A balanced body is healthy. So the body's innate tendency toward health can be harnessed to aid in the manifesting process.

The human body is constantly recreating itself. It is never "full grown," according to medical science. Different parts of the body are completely replaced cell by cell over well-known time periods. For example, medicine has determined that the skin is completely replaced every two years. The stomach lining grows anew every five days. The liver's cells are replaced by new cells every two months, and so on.[33] Obviously this process is not instant; each cell dies and is replaced one at a time so that functioning is not disrupted. But the fact of this turnover in cellular structure gives rise to a fundamental question in medicine: Why does disease or injury continue in the new cells of the body? They should be healthy because they were just manufactured by DNA and have not been exposed to disease or injury.

The answer, according to Deepak Chopra, M.D. and David Simon, M.D., in their lectures entitled *Training the Mind, Healing the Body*, is cellular memory. I would call it "soul-ular memory." Exciting research of Candace B. Pert, Ph.D.,[34] formerly with the National Institutes of Mental Health, proves that memory is stored not just in the brain but also throughout the body. Memory of a traumatic event such as illness or injury is stored in the affected body part. When new cells are manufactured the memory of illness or injury is passed on. The *memory* is passed on. Not the disease. Not the injury. The *memory* of the trauma is retained by the combined body/soul being. As Light Being soul we *manifest* that trauma in the body because that's the version of the body we remember.

We manifest what we truly and firmly believe. And most of us believe what the human senses perceive. Tomorrow morning, when you awake, you will manifest into reality precisely what you went to bed believing about your world. You do it from memory. From habit. If you are not sure about this, remember that for centuries Europeans lived on a flat Earth. They experienced our planet as flat, saw it ending at the horizon, and therefore believed Earth to be a plate. Reality stayed that way until Christopher Columbus and others disproved human perception by sailing past the horizon without falling off. In the same way, if you believe yourself to be physically injured or emotionally hurt by another's behavior you will manifest that pain in your daily reality.

Like Christopher Columbus, you can change reality with new perceptions. The memory of trauma can be released. A new memory can be created, allowing a new physical condition to result from the new cells being created. Self-healing is a reality. You can heal yourself. Now, you are saying, "I can't create a new leg once mine is cut off." Or, "I can't heal my spine or brain once it is so broken that I am paralyzed." Some of these objections are true. If the body part is completely missing, like an amputated arm or leg, you most likely will not manifest a new one. But that is not because it would defy the laws of DNA's nature. Every cell in the body is capable of reproducing an entire human body. Once science cracks that code and gives us permission to believe it is possible to grow new limbs, we will start manifesting them.

If the body structure is still intact, like the broken spine or injured brain, it is still possible to manifest self-healing. It may take the form of anything from simple improvement to complete restoration of function, depending upon your chosen goals for this lifetime. That is, if your purpose in choosing this particular life in this body was to experience what it is like to be wheelchair-bound in a society that values mobility, then you will not defeat that purpose by healing your crippled body. Or, if you intend to experience physical dependence on a loved one in this life, the illness creating that necessity may not be healed. But if the injury or illness is incidental to your main purpose in being here, you can apply your ability to manifest to effect self-healing.

The key, as always, is attention and intention. You must first turn your attention to the situation, however briefly or extensively you choose. But be careful where you place your attention. Keep in mind that constant thought on one topic manifests those thoughts into what we perceive as reality. Concentrate on the wellness of your body, not its illness.

Our society as a whole believes that illness or injury should be elevated to a position of dominating life. Medical professionals must be consulted. Scientific cures sought. Grieving must be extensive, and often, and debilitating. Family life must be disrupted to make room for the illness or injury. The loved one disappears to be replaced by a "patient" or "case," or worse, "cripple." In essence, the trauma must be magnified in proportion to the fear it generates. All of this constitutes "attention" to the situation, and is therefore a necessary part of the manifesting equation for those who believe this is the right attention to give.

Yet, some very successful self-healing is accomplished by people we accuse of being "in denial." These deranged folks do not seem to understand the drama of their situation and refuse to follow the societal standard. Instead, they hear the word "cancer" or "paralysis" and seemingly refuse to believe it. But wait. Is it that they refuse to believe the diagnosis? Or could it be they refuse to allow that diagnosis to overtake the reality they manifest? Perhaps they hear and understand the "reality" of the situation and simply choose not to follow the societal role for the ill and injured. They manifest a new path for themselves and use their "denial" to self-heal. It is not unusual for such people to ignore their cancer right into remission, or to find a way to walk when medical professionals declare it impossible. How do they do it? Maybe through the force of the second, and most important, part of the manifesting equation: intention.

Manifesting always obeys expectation—our firmly held beliefs. We experience the results of both conscious and unconscious intentions for our lives. The primary guidance for our lives as humans, of course, is the experience we seek by investing part of our Energy into a human. Our entire lives will play out so as to generate the relationship experiences we crave to further our own evolution. Within the confines of that primary guidance, however, we have immeasurably wide latitude to do as we choose. Free will. We may manifest whatever we would like to experience. Most of the time manifesting is done unconsciously, because most of us have not awakened to the knowledge of our ability to manifest. So we manifest physical reality based on past observations basically out of habit.

What would happen if you would choose to break the habit? What normally happens when you take a fresh look at something?

You have an "ah ha" moment—a new perception. Is not the purpose of looking at things differently to experience a new perception? So do it. Look at illness or emotional pain in a new way, from a different perspective, even one you do not like. Break the habit by seeing, doing, saying, feeling, learning, something different, something new. Intend to cast off the shackles of your habitual manifestations by seeking a new experience. And make that new experience an exercise in self-healing.

Where do you start? With energy. Everything in our universe is energy—Source Energy. The Energy of Source's thoughts and love. The Being of Energy within the body. *The Presence Process: A Healing Journey into Present Moment Awareness*[35] is a most excellent ten-week self-healing course that focuses the soul's healing energy. Energy-based therapies such as Network Chiropractic, Reiki, Healing Touch, somatic experiencing, and others, can also be very effective in helping you harness your own healing energy. Focus your energies on healing instead of being ill or feeling emotional pain. Focus your willpower on achieving that goal. Laser beam your whole being on the "knowing" that you can heal. Eventually you will break the memory chain, the habit of new cells duplicating the old trauma you carry around.

You can commit to self-healing whether you believe you can do it or not. You do not need to forgo the "attention" part of the equation and stop going to doctors and pursuing their treatments. Just form the mental and emotional intention to heal yourself. If you have difficulty forming this intention because your habitual belief system precludes self-healing, try accessing your innate Light Being unconditional love to envelope yourself in its healing power. Find something about your illness or emotional pain to love. That sounds impossible when you are suffering. Yet it is not. As an example, when I was consumed with fear that I had breast cancer, I had my beyond-death experience to love. Similarly, during a yearlong illness in 2001-2, when fear and pain pursued me as relentlessly as the ticking of a clock, I found meditation to love. I also loved the fact that I did not have to work. It was because I was too sick to function, but still I got out of working without feeling guilty. Find something, anything, to love about your situation. Once you find that love, use it to form the intention to heal.

Then give that healing intention your attention so that it will manifest. Formulate a plan for effecting your healing and follow that plan. Try a lot of different things until you find one or more that "click(s)" for you. Your intuition will tell you what feels right for you. Trust it. Follow its lead.

One powerful self-healing technique is to change your perception of what is normal. Oftentimes we believe we have an illness just because our physical condition departs from what we have come to recognize as normal for us. We then label that change with a judgmental connotation, such as, "I have a problem with my . . .," or, "something's wrong with me," instead of accepting that we have a much wider range in variation of what is healthy for us.

For example, if we have become accustomed to a daily "constitutional" (bowel movement), having diarrhea may seem to signal an illness when in fact the body is simply purging some absorbed toxin. We see the negative or problematic explanation before even considering that there might be a healthy one. Sometimes a "hands off" approach is the best one while our host body pursues its own innate healing wisdom.

Often, in order to heal you have to actually relive or retrace prior injuries, both physical and emotional, for a brief period of time. You feel the pain as the injuries are healing. The pain will not last as long as it originally did when you stuffed it down into your body to try to get rid of it. But because you have done this, the body has to work through and purge the pain literally out of its cells, out of its cellular memory, so you both can heal. For example, I went through this with spinal injuries in 2005-06. As muscles began to heal, I felt the pain of the automobile accident that caused my suffering. As each muscle unclenched, the muscle above it would be painful until it was able to release its burden of pain and tightness. Then the one above that would be painful. Pain marched up my spine this way inch by inch to my head. As each level of pain resolved, I would have crying spells. Grieving for things I knew about, such as pain and loss of mobility, and for things I did not know. The crying helped release the trauma and purge the emotional pain, which helped the healing process. So do not try to avoid crying or reliving old pains. If you do, you will be depriving yourself of the benefits of self-healing, and keeping your host body in a state of perpetual disease, illness, or injury that you have an obligation as the resident soul to help it resolve and heal.

Try using your creative powers to visualize your disease or injury improving. For example, a pediatric oncologist once told me he had introduced his small cancer patients to the Pac-Man arcade game and asked them to visualize Pac-men eating up their tumors. His patients have achieved some real healing success by doing this.

Finally, stop doing whatever it is that makes you sick. Using your Light Being access to Universal Knowledge will not be enough to increase your vibrational level and further your evolution if your thinker, as discussed in previous chapters, constantly bombards you with negative messages.

If your work or a relationship is killing you with stress, find new work and new relationships. If your eating habits cause physical damage, adopt a new eating plan. You cannot heal yourself while continuing toxic habits. Everyone has a story about someone who smoked three packs of cigarettes a day, consumed 4,000 fat-laden calories a day, worked a high-stress job, and then died of a heart attack, to the surprise of his family who exclaim: "But he was never sick a day in his life." Clearly he *was* sick, but was ignoring his own body's messages.

Some people understandably want to dull their senses when they come home from a long day of unhappy work. So they drink, smoke, take drugs, and otherwise chemically induce oblivion. There is a better way. The difficult parts of our day can be smoothed over by accessing our innate healing and opening ourselves to a higher vibrational level through exercising Light Being powers. Enjoy music. Exercise–the body is designed to move not lounge. Rest the body. Eat healthy whole foods. Meditate into quieting the voice in your head. Create something. Learn something. Do something for someone else, especially sending your healing energy out to others who need it. Not only will you feel better, but the world will be better for your efforts.

Use manifesting to heal old ways of thinking, old traumas, old habitual responses based on animal motivations. Then learn to consciously manifest wonderful things for yourself. Make your own dream of good health come true.

15

Stop Judging

Inherent in the animal instinct for survival is judgment, for everything must be assessed for threat potential. Everyone adjudged either friend or foe.

If our modern lifestyle lacks daily survival threats the primitive part of the brain affects the higher brain functions, resulting in risk assessments on a finer scale, such as for conformity to one's own religious or social standards. Everything and everyone is constantly screened for risks and judged according to how they fit within our own animal comfort zone. Events and behaviors are judged good or bad, right or wrong, from one perspective only—that of the self as judge. This is human nature.

Humans strive so hard to live a life of conformity because they are herd animals. Most people set the parameters of their comfort zones by what they perceive to be the tolerated range of normal. Normal meaning conformity to what most people choose. The big part of the bell curve. No one wants to be abnormal, for that is outside the herd's collective comfort zone. Schools hold students to the norms historically set for education. Parents train their children to stay within traditional behavior parameters accepted by society. Even psychiatrists adhere to the conformity model by measuring all human behavior against allegedly scientifically derived "normal" values. We strive to conform to "normal" out of fear of rejection by the herd.

Conformity may be typical animal behavior, but it becomes a myth when applied to the soul. Each of us is unique in our personality and development. Each soul has tasks to complete that may be hindered by attempts to fulfill the animal expectation of conformity to herd patterns. How, then, are we to evolve in a norm-addicted society? Stop judging what is normal.

All negative consequences of deviation from "normal" behavior can be eliminated by society if its members so choose. We can remove the stigma of being outside the norm by refusing to judge those who choose another way. Just stop judging. Stop verbally criticizing those who appear different. Stop mentally chastising them. Stop funding research into what is "normal" human behavior. Stop publishing articles, opinions, and stories about the prevalent choice made by those who were polled. In short, stop setting herd comfort zones and allow individuals to set their own without fear of reprisal or being labeled "abnormal," "weird," or "different."

Our true Energy nature is not to judge others. Why? Because as Light Beings we have the innate ability to experience events from the individual perspectives of each soul involved. We "get" the really big picture from all perspectives. We use our multiple levels of simultaneous awareness to perceive events through the senses and emotions of others. That otherworldly sensitivity proves time and again that the information available from only one perspective is far too little to make an accurate judgment.

During my own life reviews I experienced everything I said and did from the perspective of those around me at the time. Over and over I realized how wrong my perspective had been, how limited or stilted toward my own fears or self-centeredness. The evidence demonstrated way beyond a shadow of a doubt that attempts to judge events or people from within the human condition is foolish.

Exercising unconditional love during my life review allowed me to appreciate other people's levels of evolution and understand that certain behaviors are typical in various evolutionary states. It is similar to the difference in perspectives of the parent and the child. A parent would never expect a child of two years to be evolved enough to ride a bicycle. Similarly, as Light Beings, we accept certain behaviors from less evolved souls and do not judge them for acting "age" appropriately. The same holds true for every stage of evolution. Including our own. "Judge not lest ye be judged" does not mean there will be a judgment day after death in the sense religion professes. It means that engaging in the act of judging others reveals for all to see that you are at a lower evolutionary stage yourself. It discloses how far from unconditional love you live.

Your individual emotional responses, perspectives, fears, and comfort zone all result from your own experiences throughout this life and others. No one else's are identical. So what triggers a dislike or signal that something is outside your own comfort zone may be completely different than another's. For example, we may see a beggar living on the street and mentally judge him to be "disgusting," or "unfortunate," depending upon our unique perspectives. But we very definitely judge him as someone we do not want to be. Yet my understanding from beyond death is that more evolved Light Beings select more challenging lives on Earth. The bum we adjudged to be beneath us may actually be a far more highly evolved soul who volunteered to accept a life of hardship in order to teach us humility. Our human fear-based perspective has blinded us to the truth of the bum's unconditional love for us.

What blinds us even more, however, is the amnesia inherent in the human experience. We do not remember who we are or why we are here. We cannot see the interconnectedness of all of creation or the ramifications of every thought and deed. We do not see the ripples through the fabric of the universe in response to our thoughts and actions, and those of everyone else. Lacking that vision, we also lack the ability to judge accurately whether something furthers evolution or retards it. So much is going on around us that we cannot perceive that we are in the worst possible position from which to judge anything—anything other than our own animal comfort zones. So do not judge your own life or anyone else's. We cannot know while here how events unfold through the ripple effect.

For example, I was terrified of having breast cancer—an unfounded fear as it turned out. At the time I judged it to be a tragedy. I worried I had done something to deserve breast cancer, such as failing to take better care of myself, or taking birth control pills, thereby judging myself as the culprit. I blamed my law firm for putting so much stress on me, judging my partners guilty for the effects of my own relentless ambition. I could not see beforehand what a blessing the cancer scare had been, for it set the stage for my beyond-death experience, the most glorious event of this life. I will not know until my next life review whether my reaction to the local anesthesia may play a small role in replacing the needle localization procedure with a less invasive technique, thereby sparing thousands of woman the pain I endured. Nor can I see the impact this book may have on someone who reads it. What I once perceived as tragedy has improved my life immeasurably— and, just maybe, it has helped another as well.

That is the danger of judging. We are almost always wrong from a global and loving perspective, which is the only view that counts when we awaken in the Light.

Let us strive to replace judging with tolerance—tolerance of others' choices, knowing that each of us is on our own unique evolutionary path. We should offer others the same trust in their choices that we expect for our own. The same compassion for their missteps as we wish for our own. We should offer each other unconditional love--love free of judgment, free of conditions. No strings attached. Love that does not disappear when someone steps outside our comfort zone or does what we would prefer they did not.

16

✳ Treat Each Other Responsibly

As Light Beings, we have the magical ability to put ourselves in another's position, to literally see, hear, feel and think as they do in response to our own behavior. This is part of the life review process we undergo during transition back into Energy form after death of the body. We experience firsthand how our own thoughts, words, and deeds impacted those around us. More than that, in our natural Light state we can literally merge our Energy into another's, and experience the other's life as though it were our own. This is total immersion into another's beingness, another's viewpoint. It is a lesson in perspective necessary for our evolution.

While we cannot physically merge Energies while in human form, the version of this ability we retain in the body gives us an understanding of and compassion for others. What do most of us do with our ability to "walk a mile in [another's] shoes?" We throw it away. We *choose* to act like an animal, either ignoring the consequences of our behavior, or, worse, blaming our victims.

In the United States we have institutionalized irresponsible behavior in our laws and daily interactions. Our laws allow polluters to disperse specified amounts of poisons, automobile manufacturers to continue certain safety violations, drug companies to kill and maim a certain percentage of their consumers, and tobacco companies to continue selling a product proven to eventually injure everyone who uses it. Oh, these companies have to "walk a mile" in their victims' shoes when they get sued. But even then juries steeped in the tradition of irresponsibility allow many violations to go unredressed, or they award the victims only money, as though money could restore health.

Americans take so little responsibility for their own actions that millions of dollars have to be spent annually putting obvious warning labels on products in an attempt to avoid lawsuits by, for example, a woman who is careless with hot coffee and a family that chooses to eat fattening food but wants to blame someone else for it.

Irresponsibility and lack of compassion have become so ingrained in our culture that even therapists and counselors sometimes blame their own clients for their emotional pain without even realizing they are doing it. A popular piece of psychological advice today is roughly paraphrased, "no one can hurt you unless you let him/her." This is often followed by the advice: "Don't give away your power to the other person by being hurt." A close look at this advice discloses that it fits into the animal model of behavior, instead of Light Being compassion.

As an example, let us examine the joke of a male, Bob, telling his wife, Sally, "you look fat in that dress." This is an interaction often used to characterize the differences between male and female perspectives.

Sally may be advised, "Don't give away your power to Bob by letting his comment hurt you." Right away, looking at the words being used here, "power" and "letting" words hurt you, reveals that the advice is based upon the animal fearful/hierarchical view of the world. Sally is depicted as a loser. She has lost the "power" she and Bob are allegedly competing for in their relationship. And she has failed in the competition because she "let" Bob hurt her. Bob is the winner because he gets "power" over Sally's emotions. Apparently any type of power, no matter how small, has value in this model of life.

Similarly, Sally may be told, "Bob can't hurt you unless you let him." If this is true, and Sally is hurt by Bob's comment, then according to this "truth," it is her own fault. She is a failure for allowing Bob's rudeness to hurt her. Sally has done nothing but *hear* the insult. Yet, according to this model for behavior, she is responsible for her own injury instead of Bob. The blame for Bob's bad behavior has been shifted to the victim. Bob, on the other hand, scores big. He puts Sally down (thereby getting "one-up" on her), seizes the "power" to hurt her feelings, and bears no responsibility for the consequences of his behavior because Sally gets full blame for feeling hurt.

Do you see how this plays out as a fearful model of life? Bob has competed for one-upmanship over Sally in a world where every interaction is a competition for being "on top," and, he has avoided being pushed around by pushing first. This is animal behavior. Sally, who may approach life by establishing connections and consensus, has lost not only closeness with Bob, but also confirmation of her self-worth and support for her creative efforts to dress up. Her attempts to act from Light Being motivations have been ridiculed.

And this advice is routinely given in today's society!

Those who justify this advice might say that Sally needs to build up her own self-esteem so she is no longer wounded by Bob's insults. She needs to "toughen up" and "take it like a man." Clearly, this justification comes from a fearful and male model of the world. It is precisely this kind of thinking that has created our current culture of self-centered humans with no compassion at all for each other. This attitude is filling our therapists' offices, psychiatric institutions, and prisons. For the less we as a society value each other's emotions the more animal-like we become.

Proponents of the advice could also argue that Sally has several choices. She can avoid Bob and his insults (hard to do if she is married to him). She can defend herself by playing along with the male perspective of competition. However, if she chooses this option, Sally becomes responsible for more of her own hurt caused by what is said in the argument if she cannot successfully "one up" Bob and take back the "power." Or, Sally can choose to change her perspective on the situation, with the result that she is no longer hurt by Bob's insult. Sally takes back the "power" by robbing Bob of his one-upmanship points for the insult because it was not effective in putting her down. All these justifications focus on how to better play the fearful world-view game, which still puts the burden of having hurt feelings on Sally as though emotions were a curse.

But feelings are not a curse! They are one of the primary reasons Light Beings like us choose to blend into a human body. We crave a multitude of human experiences to feel not only the physical sensations they generate but also the emotional ones. Emotions are innate, like instincts, and cannot be eliminated through control or otherwise. Adopting a psychological position that punishes a person for having hurt feelings, while letting the one whose behavior choice caused the injury to go scot-free, cannot get farther away from the higher vibrational stages we must attain in order to evolve.

A variation of this blame game might be to blame Sally for asking Bob's opinion in the first place, inasmuch as she probably already knows he will say something hurtful. Once again, this puts the burden on the victim, and absolves the wrongdoer of responsibility for his conduct. More than that, it enables Bob to continue to be inconsiderate—perhaps unknowingly so.

A more loving piece of advice would be to suggest to Sally that she tell Bob his comment is hurtful. That type of comment *is* objectively hurtful. There is nothing wrong with Sally that turned it into an insult. It was framed and intended to be hurtful by Bob. Sally was merely the passive recipient. Sally needs to be aware of her feelings and have the courage to express them to Bob. Bob's job is not to agree or disagree with Sally's feelings. He may wish to explain his behavior, but he has no right to tell Sally that her feelings are wrong or unjustified. Sally's challenge then becomes one of determining, after hearing Bob's explanations, whether she in fact overreacted, and what part she may have played in the conflict (such as, did she ask Bob whether she looked fat in the dress in order to provoke a fight).

Bob's responsibility is to accept Sally's feelings as valid, then analyze what he could have done differently to avoid hurting her. We all must learn that it goes against both human and Light Being desires to feel hurt. Rarely does one choose it consciously. In fact, Bob may simply be acting out various hurts suffered during childhood or carried over into this life from other ones. Still, Bob must take responsibility for his current behavior, apologize, and train himself not to make insulting comments again.

Long term, Sally must let go of the hurt, heal herself, and try to work with Bob to overcome what might have become an ingrained pattern for them both. In this way, each supports the other, and both evolve toward a more aware, more supportive, and more loving relationship. Compassion has replaced fear, and the cycle of fear and pain has been broken, ultimately bringing both parties more peace and happiness in the marriage. Accessing Light Being nature has solved the problem.

The Bob and Sally example contains an objectively hurtful insult, and should not be confused with the situation where no overt insult is made, but one is projected into the situation by one party to the interchange. Take the example of a graphic designer and publisher. The graphic designer had been commissioned to create the cover of a new book. She produced a result she loved and felt she had done her best. The publisher, who also loved the cover design, nevertheless requested a redesign. The designer was insulted.

The publisher's desire to redesign the cover was not intrinsically insulting. It could have been he just wanted to go another way, or perhaps the market had changed, making another design more saleable. There are a number of reasons why the publisher might want a different cover design, none of which reflect any insult to the graphic designer's work. The graphic designer *read the insult into* the situation because of a self-esteem issue, or unresolved childhood beliefs about her abilities, or because she was emotionally invested in the design she created.

Let us change the facts a bit and say the publisher rejected the design saying it was "amateurish, sloppy, and totally unrelated to the content of the book." Now the insult is intrinsic in the rejection. The words themselves are as hurtful as the rejection. More than that, they are aimed personally at the designer and seek to belittle or demean her as an artist and professional. In this scenario feeling insulted is normal human emotion.

From a pure Light Being perspective, however, no insult would be felt because there would be no element of human ego to perceive it. A Light Being in its natural state would recognize the insult, but not take it personally, because it would know that the publisher is evolving on his own path in his own way and at his own speed. A Light Being would merely observe that the publisher had much to learn about how to show respect for others, and would love him unconditionally anyway. Acting from that higher level, we might choose to drop the matter of the insult entirely, or use it as an entree into a discussion that might bring significant growth and evolution to the publisher.

Unfortunately, we are not in our pure Light state while acting as souls, so we share human emotions. We are here specifically to experience what having sensitive emotions is like, and how to have relationships with others despite them. So we must learn to respect our bodies' emotions, and those of others, and give consideration to them in our daily interactions. That cannot be done in a society that prizes exerting power over emotions and manipulating people by using their emotions against them.

We must deconstruct our blame-the-victim society: first, by focusing awareness on this animal-based habit and the fact that it has been institutionalized; then, by teaching everyone a more responsible and compassionate way to interrelate. "Do unto others as you would have them do unto you" is a very sound philosophy and teaching tool, for it forces you to move your perspective out of your fear or anger toward another and into their emotional environment. It brings you a little closer to your true nature as a Being of Light.

If we work together, we can stop this vicious cycle of distrust and disrespect. But we must each be the first to take responsibility for our actions, treat others responsibly, and show compassion regardless of whether it is returned. Why? Because new behaviors always start with the enlightened among us.

17

Manifest Consciously

As children, we all dreamed of growing up to change the world some day. That dream was not childish. Nor was it misplaced. But it has been forgotten. We *can* change the world through our thoughts, through manifesting, through exploring and expanding our natural Light Being abilities while here on Earth. We have simply forgotten we can. Michael Brown explains how this has happened most eloquently in *The Presence Process*:

> Whenever the effects of our thoughts, words, and deeds are significantly delayed by time, they appear to us to occur independently of any cause. The consequence is that we then assume that many of the circumstances of our life are happening *to us* and not *because of us*. This enables us to enter victim or victor mentality. Being a victim or a victor means that we are either complaining about our experiences or competing with the experiences of others. Because of the pauses between cause and effect manufactured by time, it never occurs to us that we are actually complaining about ourselves and the consequences of our own actions, or that we are actually competing with ourselves because of the obstacles that we have placed in our own way. Being a victim or victor is no different than the behavior of a dog chasing its own tail. The only difference is that the dog has more fun.

Reactive behavior is founded on a belief that the world is happening *to* us and that it is therefore our duty to enforce our will upon it. This illusion appears to be real to us only because we are "living in time." Living in time is an unconscious state in which our attention is almost exclusively focused on our past and on the future that we have projected for ourselves. The consequence of this unconscious state is that, for the most part, the distance between our thoughts, words, and deeds and their inevitable physical, mental, and emotional consequences is just long enough for us to be able to convince ourselves that we are not the cause of most of our present life experiences.[36]

As integral parts of Source, we souls continuously manifest our experience of the physical world around us. All those millions of random thoughts coursing through your mind every day affect you in a big way, and everything else in the universe to a smaller degree, once they are formed—and even more so if believed.

We can increase awareness of our own manifesting through the simple expedient of *noticing* our lives. Focusing our attention and intention on being present in the moment. Observing. Being alive right now and opening ourselves up to really sensing everything around us. Noticing the connection between something we may have thought, and then experienced, such as the common phenomenon of thinking about someone and then having them call. Notice how often you say to someone, "I was just thinking about you."

Society has taught us to both ignore our manifestations and to renounce responsibility for them. This is an excellent example of our use of the human trait of denial. We ignore our own manifestations, and those of our co-creators, simply by virtue of the fact that it is human nature to block out awareness of most of what we observe. Take a simple example of sitting on a park bench in autumn. Do you usually notice the feel of cool hardness of the bench you sit on, or the asphalt below the soles of your shoes? Do the sounds of children playing, crisp autumn leaves crunching as people walk over them, the wind whipping through tree limbs, or squawking birds flying in formation overhead normally grab your attention? What about the smell of your own cologne or the pungent moldy smell of soil and browning leaves? Do you notice them? If you are like most of us, you would be wrapped up in your own thoughts instead of paying any attention at all to sensory input from your surroundings. We have all trained our minds to ignore most of what the body is telling us. We have blanketed ourselves in the denial of human nature.

What happens when we set aside the denial and focus entirely on the present moment? The sensory data comes into awareness. You notice your external environment. And, in doing so, you can become aware of your own manifestations and those of your co-creators.

Let us go back to the park bench example and assume you focused your attention and intention earlier in the day on finding a reliable babysitter for your children. You sit on the bench stewing over how you are going to find that babysitter. You mentally make lists of places to look, people to ask, and ideas for finding just the right person. In the meantime, the perfect person sits one bench over reading the want ads. You have manifested your own solution but have been too steeped in denial of your surroundings to even see the results. Your human habit of blocking out the present moment has forced you to ignore the woman you used to admire as your neighbor's babysitter sitting right beside you.

More often than failing to recognize the results of our manifesting, we fail to take credit for them. We pray for what we want as though something external to the one Source of which we are a part has exclusive power to answer our prayers. Because Source is not separate from us, we are in reality praying to ourselves as the Collective Being I call Source. Yet when we actually strip off the denial, and open our awareness to see the fruits of our manifesting, we call it "coincidence," "fluke," or "good luck." Or maybe we proclaim it to be an "omen" or "sign." The more religious among us say: "Our prayers have been answered." We refuse to take responsibility or credit for our own manifestations *because we do not believe we can manifest reality.* We believe God can manifest reality but mistakenly assume we are not part of that God/Source. In fact, we are simply extensions of Source with the same abilities. We can and do manifest our own lives as we go along. We do it completely unconsciously based on our beliefs.

Our beliefs also manifest who we are—our soul personality as well as our human's. Children demonstrate this every day. Parents may devote considerable time and energy to raising a child to believe he is wonderful and precious. That child repeats the parents' words as his own thoughts, eventually creating a belief in self-worth. Take that same child and put him in kindergarten with children who repeatedly mock his body weight, or even just avoid him without a word, and eventually the precious child comes to believe he is unworthy. His thinker replays the children's taunts and rejection as he cries into his pillow. Over and over the precious child tells himself that he is fat and unlovable. He comes to believe it. That self-view now defines the child, who thereafter continues to manifest his own life to perpetuate it. Kindergarten children co-created a human personality consumed with fear of others who might mock or shun him, as well as a soul burdened with the pain of self-loathing. Kindergarten children! Such is the power of thoughts. Theirs. And his.

It is time to admit to ourselves that we do manifest, alone, and in concert with those around us. More importantly, it is time to begin taking responsibility for our creations by starting to manifest on a conscious level. How? The same way we are doing it now—with our thoughts and beliefs. All we need to do is be present in the moment and direct our attention and intention to the process.

First, we must pay attention to our own thoughts. Assume the "watcher" position and make your mind a blank. Assign yourself the task of manifesting for a particular purpose and observe the "thinker." For example, assume your home has been taken by the County through eminent domain to construct a highway and you must find another house costing no more than $50,000. Actually notice what pops into your mind. Do you say to yourself, "I'll never find another house I can afford?" Or, "It's impossible to find something this time of year that quickly?" Are your thoughts immediately negative? Fearful? If you continue to think that way you may well manifest a negative outcome.

If your thoughts follow a more positive note, do they run something like, "if God wills it, we'll find a house?" Or, "if it's supposed to happen, it will?" These thoughts are more hopeful, yet they assume you are powerless to affect the events of your own life. You are not powerless. We each have the exact same power to manifest reality—consciously or unconsciously.

Push all thoughts back out of your mind again. This time, instead of waiting for your thinker to fill your mind, consciously form the intention: "We will find the right home for us." Follow with, "the home for us is out there and we will find it in time." Notice the lack of specificity of the wording. "Home" can mean any type of shelter, not necessarily a $50,000 house you purchase. Leaving your intention open-ended allows others more leeway to manifest jointly with you and still meet their own needs. Repeat these phrases, or some semblance of them, over and over whenever negative or hopeful but powerless thoughts spring to mind. This represents the "intention" part of the manifesting equation.

Then do the legwork as the "attention" phase. Go out and get a realtor to look for you. Cruise neighborhoods likely to have houses in your price range. Look in the newspapers ads. Go on the Internet to the realtor websites. Keep your attention and intention aligned by thinking and working the solution into reality.

After some time, you will begin to notice "coincidences" relating to your need to find a new house. An old friend will call and tell you she just got her realtor's license. A house in your price range will suddenly come on the market and have to be sold quickly because someone had to move unexpectedly to another state. Or, the County Engineer dies and the new one wants to reroute the highway. These may all be solutions you have manifested in co-creation with others. You did not cause the County Engineer to die, for instance. The other participants in the events that could solve your problem manifested as they did because it fit within their own evolutionary path.

You may say you have tried this process many times and it did not work. If that is the case, there may be one or more impediments at work—all of which you also manifested.

First, we manifest only what we *truly* believe—*subconsciously* truly believe, as well as consciously believe. Regardless of how skilled we are at manifesting in the body, we will not manifest something that defies our beliefs. For example, no matter how much attention and intention you put into trying to produce abundance, you will not open a kitchen drawer and magically find a wad of cash there. Why not? Because you do not believe money grows in a kitchen drawer. You believe money has to be earned or gifted to you. And, while you may believe that someone could give you a wad of cash, you are not inclined to accept that the tooth fairy will put it in your kitchen drawer. So align your attention and intention with your beliefs. Leave your intention open to receiving any form of abundance and then watch for it to come in a form that matches your beliefs—say, an old friend who has owed you money for 20 years suddenly pays you back. That you can believe.

Second, the events you did manifest matched your beliefs, but you did not recognize it because you lack self-awareness. Self-awareness—intimate knowledge of you as the Light Being you truly are and as the soul of a human being—is essential to successful manifesting while in the body. That includes awareness of your total belief system, including the unconscious ones formed before you reached the "age of reason" of seven years. It includes all the emotional beliefs about yourself of which you may be completely unaware.

For example, a woman may devote considerable energy to trying to manifest "Mr. Right" into her life. At the same time, she may subconsciously *truly* believe that she does not deserve the type of man she has envisioned. Because she suffered emotional abuse at the hands of her father, this poor woman may believe the best she deserves is someone who will put her down, insult her, and emotionally berate her like her father did. What type of man do you think she will meet time after time? The belief must change before the manifesting will. Our lady will have to put the effort into resolving her emotional pain, accepting the wonder of who she truly is, and reconstructing her self-esteem before she will be able to manifest a Mr. Right who will treat her as she should be treated.

Third, you may have tried manipulation instead of manifestation. Some spiritual gurus proclaim that all you have to do is visualize anything you want and it will come to you without effort. They may actually believe that giving attention and intention to a fantasy picture, perhaps supported by positive verbalizations or affirmations, constitutes manifestation. But it does not. Manifesting is an innate natural ability we have as Beings of Light. It is not a magic act. Nor is it a trick we can pull on the universe. We manifest because we *are Source*. And as such, our manifestations arise from our evolutionary path back to the Source. If that path does not include wealth, we will not manifest it in our human lives. And no amount of trying to manipulate the universe into producing wealth for us will work. We use our innate Light character only to further our evolution. It is not a magic wand to change the circumstances of the human experience we came here to have.

If you have any question in your mind about whether you are trying to manipulate instead of manifest, try boosting your overall receptivity to Light Being nature by consciously choosing to engage in more evolved activities. For example, rather than watch a football game on TV, which is entertaining but essentially competitive animal behavior, watch a creative drama or listen to music. Instead of fighting with your spouse or children when you get upset, read a book that reminds you of your spiritual nature. Meditate. Spend alone time thinking and doing nothing, with no outside stimulus or noise, so that you as Light Being sense that you as soul are willing to listen and hear. Use a self-awareness program to discover your hidden motivations—those harmful beliefs about yourself that keep producing manifestations designed to focus your attention on unresolved emotional wounds. Put in the hard work necessary to evolve. You are never going to manifest your way around it anyway.

Finally, practice monitoring your thoughts and train your thinker to eliminate negative attitudes that spring from negative beliefs about yourself. When you catch yourself worrying that the boss is going to read you the riot act, immediately shift your thought to: "The boss will understand what happened and not criticize me for it." As the thought, "I hate that guy," forms in your mind, change it to: "That guy's ok, even though we don't see eye-to-eye." And when your inner voice starts calling you names like "stupid," or "fat," block it with self-loving thoughts of what a great and powerful Light Being you are, and how evolved you must be to have chosen such a challenging human life for yourself.

Positive thinking truly does work because it is our very nature to create reality through thoughts. Moreover, it slowly but surely changes our beliefs about who we truly are. Positive thinking then allows us to manifest more positive realities for ourselves in line with our new positive beliefs about ourselves. As we believe, so shall we manifest.

Do not get discouraged. Most of the time our most coveted manifestations are slow to appear, or at least for us to notice them. The more you practice, and the more aware you become of what is around you, the more often you will be able to say to yourself, "I manifested that."

As you develop your spiritual awareness share the wealth. We co-create with all other Sourcebeams. So, when our positive thoughts relate to another, or many others, they create more positive ripples through the fabric of our Oneness. Manifest what is best for the Earth and others in the same way you do for yourself. Put your intention into the universe to help solve Earth's pollution problems, give a loved one the support he needs, reduce crime in your city—anything that might lead us all forward in unconditional love. Perhaps you cannot personally do anything to solve pollution, crime, or the problem your loved one is having, but you can use your attention and intention to share loving co-creating.

18

✳ Light Up Religious Institutions

So many of our misperceptions about life flow from one central erroneous belief: that God/Source thinks and acts like a human being. Most of our religious institutions are founded upon this principle, and for that reason fail to adequately prepare us for this life or further our evolution in eternal life. Religion also swirls around a core belief in a system of rewards and punishments at the hand of a judgmental Deity. Rules of conduct have been written and interpreted in an effort to guide us to act "rightly," and dire consequences, even Hell, have been predicted for those who fail.

These centuries-old religious dogmas reflect centuries-old human perceptions of what anonymous writers who lived thousands of years ago communicated of their thoughts and beliefs. All of creation has evolved considerably since then. Yet our most basic religious tenets have not. Near-death experiencers have brought us new insights into Universal Knowledge, but their messages have not been incorporated into mainstream religions. My own beyond-death experience has convinced me that we must evolve mankind's core religious beliefs into alignment with Universal Knowledge in order to return the collective human evolutionary vibration to a frequency that will again further evolution of both body and soul.

We Must Revise Our View of God. The most fundamental backwards concept we humans cling to is our misunderstanding of the nature of God/Source. The basic truth is:

Source is not human-like.
Only souls are like Source, not human bodies.

Source is nothing like a human being, and therefore should not be portrayed as having human character traits or represented pictorially with a humanoid body. Source resembles a human about as much as electricity does. And until we can rid ourselves of the humanoid construct our religions will always miss the mark.

One major antiquated aspect of religious tradition arising from this misperception is worship. If by worship we mean giving honor and glory to God/Source, it makes sense to humans because that kind of behavior *works* with humans. But Source is not human! It does not give or withhold anything from us—either as blessings or punishments, or just to be frivolous. The Source I experienced neither needs nor desires worship. Vanity and self-aggrandizement are human traits, not Source's.

More importantly, worship is structured in a way that reinforces the belief that Source is a Being separate and apart from us, which makes us feel alone. That sense of isolation from Source makes our lives here on Earth a form of living hell, and helps form the basis for our belief that we *are* our human hosts rather than part of

Source.

I believe those parts of church services devoted to praising Source could integrate Universal Knowledge if the concept of worship were expanded to emphasize the truth that all of us are part of Source. By focusing worship on Source as a Collective Being, all souls could be reminded of their oneness with it. Loneliness would be diminished. Self-esteem would rise, and with it love. Love of Source. Love of self. Love of others. The bliss associated with that love could significantly raise the vibration of all who attend such a service. And, more unconditional love in the world would result in better behaviors with more desirable outcomes.

Another truth-based group activity for religions would be sharing gratitude for this wonderful and magical opportunity to participate in the human experience. Showing gratitude to Source for manifesting this experience for us. Being grateful to humans for offering themselves as living hosts to us souls. Proclaiming gratitude for all of creation and the Source's act of love and curiosity in manifesting it. We should concentrate on learning to live our lives as an on-going demonstration of gratitude, thereby constantly raising our own and each other's vibration level and assisting evolution. Religions could help us do this by replacing supplication for grace and gifts with gratitude for what we already have.

We Must Update Our Beliefs About How to Get

into Heaven. The Source I experienced does not want humans to sacrifice themselves or others in misguided attempts to gain its favor or a place in Heaven. Unconditional love extends throughout Source's Collective Being, including us. So there is no need whatsoever to curry favor with Source. We already have far more favor than we could imagine in our wildest dreams. Just as when you sleep the only destination upon awakening is the state we call being awake, the only destination upon awakening from this human experience is life as the spiritual Being of Light you are. Our destination after death of the human body is awakening into the unconditional love of the Source—no matter what we do.

Sacrifice, whether it is giving up candy for Lent or slaying a virgin on a stone alter, is not only unnecessary but also contrary to our natural evolution. Sacrifice is offered in an attempt to manipulate Source into giving one of its extensions, one soul, what that soul thinks it wants. Manipulation is a human personality trait. As souls we have no need for it because we already know intuitively that we have the ability to manifest whatever we truly need to further our development. Performing acts of manipulation lowers the combined body/soul vibration to the slower human one, thereby retarding evolution. It also creates a dangerous role model for life by conveying the message that manipulation is acceptable behavior.

I wish religions would abandon the whole concept of sacrifice motivated by the desire for a self-serving result. Sacrifice to help another person, such as giving money to the poor, is a wonderful act that benefits our Collective Being so long as the motive is love. Its beneficial effect is lost, however, when given in the hopes of Earthly or spiritual reward. For example, asking people to sacrifice to build a grander church, just for grandeur's sake, is an act of human ego. Magnificent church buildings tend to say, "Look at how pious and holy we are and how much we give to worship God." That serves only the human desire for recognition through competition. Source is *inside* and throughout us. No outward edifice holds the exclusive key to communion with Source. Churches offer us places of refuge where we can be comfortable with our spirituality and bond with other spiritual people. We should honor churches for that. But opulence is unnecessary.

Instead of acts of sacrifice, religious observances could incorporate Light Being characteristics by featuring acts of joy. Spiritual events centered on joy would raise the vibration of all concerned. Those churches and other groups who sing and dance in joy are on the right track.

We Must Create Our Own Behavior Code. Religious codes of conduct were originally designed to give guidance on how to live a spiritual life in a physical body. But that purpose has been discarded by so many. A large percentage of Earth's inhabitants have lost hope, and so believe it does not matter what they do to themselves or others. Another large percentage believes they must follow a prescribed set of rules in order to be saved. Yet they do not follow them. Ancient religious guiding principles have been abandoned in favor of an "every man for himself" attitude.

What the body and soul need for their own respective evolutions can be found *inside* the combined body/soul entity. Nothing out there anywhere is as relevant. Each soul knows best what types of experiences it seeks. Human nature likewise includes intuitive knowledge of how to interrelate to enhance group survival, for humans are first and foremost herd animals. How wonderful it would be if all of us could be taught how to access this information inside on a consistent basis, instead of being told how to live by someone on the outside. Religion is where this could be taught. Our religious institutions have a unique opportunity to train us in meditation techniques, in self-examination, and in how to create codes of behavior for ourselves that foster self-love and integrity.

If an agreed upon behavior code would be helpful in group relations, evolution would be furthered by religions adopting principles of behavior that accentuate those human and Light Being traits that reduce the conflict between body and soul, and that smooth the relationships among those of us who share this Earth. For example, one such code might be:

Act from LOVE always.

Know that we are all just one being, and act as though everything you think, do, say, and feel is shared by all.

Remember that thoughts have POWER, so try to think positively and kindly.

Listen to your heart, for it will tell you what hurts and heals.

Understand that there will be conflicts between human and soul natures, and try to see each being's motivations clearly so you can resolve the conflict.

Self-defined groups like religious institutions could collectively draft a code like the one above to serve as an ideal to which members aspire. Religions already have similar codes of conduct that help us relate better to one another that can be used as starting points. The simplest example is the Golden Rule, "Do unto others as you would have them do unto you." Some of the Ten Commandments also emphasize interpersonal relations, such as, "Honor thy father and they mother", and "Thou shalt not commit adultery."

Failure to be letter-perfect in following one's own code should not be viewed as anything more than a temporary example of how difficult it is to act from the soul when encased in a human body with its own personality and drives.

Spiritual centers like churches should be places of tranquility, acceptance, accommodation, and understanding. And they could teach us all how to open our hearts to all of creation, love all human variations, and humble ourselves to the exalted position of equality in Source.

Part III - What Happens When We Die?

19

Death as a Process

We don't die. Ever. What we do is fully awaken to our own true nature as incredible, powerful, spiritual beings. My beyond-death experience proved this to me.

Only the human body undergoes the process we call death. You, the personality that you know as yourself, will *never* die because you are not your body. Your body will ultimately cease to exist as physical matter. You and your personality will *not* cease to exist and will continue to live as a Being of Light, just as you did before joining with the human body. You will *not* lose your loved ones to death. They will live on and on, eternally, as the same people you love. Only their physical form will change into pure Energy.

Death has no place in your life other than as the glorious process of reawakening to your blissful natural state as a Being of Light. What you will lose in that process is fear, pain, and the limitations and restrictions of a human body. You do not lose your identity or memories. The body's death releases its grip on you so you can "come to," as though coming out of anesthesia or a coma, and remember who and what you really are.

My own experience taught me that what humans call death is not a fixed point in time, but rather two separate and different orderly processes followed independently by body and soul. But only the body dies. The human being, a bundle of systems of energized or living dense matter, ultimately evolves back into its chemical composition. This completes the cycle of human life, from a dot of DNA in living protoplasm to the byproducts of decomposition. You as soul, on the other hand, the *real you*, continue on eternally, rejoining the Energy form you held before you chose to inhabit the body. Each being thus follows a life cycle inherent in its nature.

The Body's Dying Process. Human culture has demanded definitions of death for medical and legal purposes, forcing both fields to pinpoint a phenomenon far bigger than the head of a pin. *Stedman's Medical Dictionary* (25th ed.) defines the term "death" as "the cessation of life . . . in man, manifested by the loss of heartbeat, by the absence of spontaneous breathing, and by cerebral death."[37] *Webster's New Collegiate Dictionary* defines "death" as "a permanent cessation of all vital functions; the end of life."[38] Clearly, *Webster*'s definition more accurately portrays the event so far as the body is concerned, because it uses the modifier "permanent." It is the "permanent" element of this definition that is defied by every near-death experiencer. These definitions attempt to establish a single cutoff point in what we have always known to be the *body's* dying process.

The body will absorb the physical impact of any illness or injury causing death, including the pain. You as soul may choose to experience these events for so long as you wish to remain joined with the human being. A soul has the ability to leave the body at any time, and frequently does so spontaneously when the body is severely damaged or suffering overwhelming pain or fear.[39] Millions of near-death accounts confirm this. You therefore do not have to fear the body's death, for you can escape the physical suffering by getting out of body.

The body's natural dying process may take hours, days, or weeks. Medical examiners tell us that individual parts of the body continue to show signs of life to a certain extent even after what we call death occurs. Cells continue to live until their cellular fuel dissipates. Eventually the body returns to its natural elements through an evolutionary process we call decay. The human lifecycle, like that of all animals, is a natural and beautiful part of the ebb and flow of the universe the Source created. It is, however, completely irrelevant to what happens to you.

The Soul's Transition Process. While the human body is dying, you yourself begin an exciting metamorphosis. The transition from being a soul inhabiting a human body back to a Being of Light in its natural state requires what humans would perceive as time, and what Light Beings perceive as developmental stages in a continuous timeless process. My experience was a compassionate, comforting protocol, lovingly designed to allow the newly discarnate soul to gently and gradually allow the effects of having been in a human body to wear off, like an anesthetic wears off. While each soul's process is unique, just as each life is unique, the balance of Part III describes my own death and life in the Light as an example.

Souls relatively new to the process may experience each transition stage for long periods of what we would call time. For the soul it just seems like a state of being with no time component. Some souls may short circuit some, or even most, of the stages, as I did, because their familiarity with the process allows for a more rapid transformation. Others would appear to us to be stuck at a particular stage of transition until they are ready and willing to move on. Each soul is supported and coddled through the process in a manner best suited to that individual personality and its developmental stage.

The process of transformation upon death of the body appears to include some or all of the following steps, though not necessarily in this order:

Getting Out of Body. At the outset, you will leave your human host in order to increase your vibration or Energy signature enough to begin the process of returning to your natural state as a Light Being. The pulling out or sinking sensation I experienced during my death was me as soul separating from the body (next chapter). Others have experienced it as an escape through the top of their head, or from the head and chest. Hospice workers sometimes perceive a mist or fog rising out of the dying body. The essence leaving the body, whether seen or unseen, is the soul beginning its glorious journey back home. That soul is *you*. Your personhood is contained in that invisible spirit, not in the human's body.

Apparently getting out of the body can be a difficult choice for some, despite intense pain and suffering. At this stage, human animal fear and survival instinct quite naturally fight the process. At times like this, the dying may perceive deceased loved ones near them who appear to be coaxing them out of the body and into following them into the Light. But this is not a universal phenomenon.

The next stage of transition could be experienced as a sensation of darkness or a black void. This may simply be the newly emerged soul's perception of the separation process, similar to that of the fetus leaving the womb, during which the lack of human sensory input translates into blackness. Or it may just take a few moments for the soul to acclimate to the new environment outside the body, like the temporary blindness we all experience walking into a dark movie theater. That is how I experienced it. I could tell I was standing right in front of my body but I could not see anything.

The dark void stage is meant to be momentary. For most it is. Some souls, however, do not adjust well to the blackness and they panic. This is particularly true if the newly freed soul does not instantly see the Light. It can be a very frightening experience when the void is as far as the soul progresses before rejoining the body, as sometimes happens to near-death experiencers. Human panic may have distracted the soul from proceeding with its transformation.

A few near-death experiencers have reported terrifying excursions into the black void. My understanding is that their fearful thoughts instantly manifested into hellish realities. These tortured souls sometimes return to the body with a belief that there is no afterlife, or worse, that they have proven the existence of hell. Their experiences are absolutely valid and real. Yet, I believe that had they continued through the process, they would have progressed through the terrifying stages to be drawn into the Light.

One of the most oft-repeated features of a near-death experience is awareness of being out of body and watching Earth life from an invisible vantage point. Many near-death accounts include the soul's observation of resuscitation efforts on the human it just departed, or even tales of travel, flying across vast distances to witness friends' and families' activities the dying human could not possibly have seen. These souls have already begun to recapture their natural state of pure Energy form, as well as some of their natural spiritual abilities, including 360° vision and the ability to "be" at any level of awareness upon which their attention focuses.

Most souls who reach this stage either return to the body or notice the Light and are drawn to it. Some souls skip this stage, as I did, and go into the Light directly from the black void. What happens during an out-of-body experience depends upon how the soul focuses its attention, which itself may be a product of how painful or painless the death is. An interest in what is happening around the body may shift the soul's attention to Earthly matters, delaying awareness of the Light. This may be one of the reasons many report seeing deceased loved ones beckoning to them from the Light. These helper Light Beings appear to the dying to gently guide their awareness to the transition process they must follow.

Into the Light. Eventually all of us "see the Light," as the saying goes. We take varying amounts of time finding our ways from the body to the Light, sometimes taking time to explore Earth life as a spirit. Some travel a celestial journey or glide up a tunnel of various descriptions. The descriptions vary to reflect our creativity in manifesting. But the Light always calls to us, beckoning us like moths to the flame.

This is not the kind of light we perceive with human eyes. My understanding is that we initially perceive the higher vibrational state of the first part of the transformation as a sensation of Light. It is similar to the human awakening process in that the first perception after the blackness of sleep is light. The Light experienced after death of the body is the most incredibly bright and beautiful illumination I have ever known. It is warm, and comforting, and literally filters through our very beings to bathe us in unconditional love and acceptance.

The Light seems to mark a threshold between realms, or dimensions, or just levels of awareness. I believe it to be part of our natural spiritual "environment", to the extent that we have a natural environment. The Light is not *literally* a place, as we understand that term while in human form. The Light is more the awareness of our eternal connectedness to the Source, as well as a state of higher vibration or energy signature. Being in the Light is like returning to normal after a long illness; feeling like our old selves again. Recovery. Awakening. Coming HOME.

Once in the Light, we transform from the larval stage of human souls to wonderful butterflies of Light Beings through a process whereby we slowly, little-by-little, shake loose the emotions, amnesia, and physiological restrictions imposed by human life.

Initial Awakening Processes. While the Light nourishes us, we begin to regain some of our Light Being powers and natural abilities. These include multiple simultaneous levels of awareness, bouts of unsolicited "knowing," and the ability to instantly manifest reality, as I experienced and describe in Chapter 20.

Perhaps it is this ability to instantly manifest reality that results in so many different NDE experiencers' descriptions of Heaven and being in the Light. Inasmuch as newly released souls' most recent experiences are human, they continue that pattern and project human constructs onto and into this temporarily unfamiliar dimension. Old human expectations, hopes, and fears instantly manifest into physical reality when in the Light. Therefore, if you expect religious icons, you will see what your religion has taught you. You will visualize the Pearly Gates or other religious concepts of Heaven. If you have always imagined heaven to be a beautiful Earth scene, or a crystal city, or some other visual image, you will manifest that image as your reality until you shift your thoughts to something else or enter later stages of the process.

Light Beings who assist us through the transition from human mode to full Energy state regularly manifest realities with and for us. Reading multiple near-death experience accounts can give the impression that each experiencer went to a different place, for they all describe wondrous, though predominantly Earthly, environments. Theologians and researchers may theorize that the lack of a uniform description results from souls crossing over into different parts of an enormous afterlife landscape. And, much as Earth can be described as lush flatlands, mountains, dessert, ocean, or ice-covered, depending on where you stand, they assume afterlife travelers' reports describe different aspects of Heaven based upon where they enter. In fact, it is the soul itself, or Light Being guides co-creating with the newly passed soul, manifesting comforting environments relevant to that particular soul that accounts for the diversity of descriptions. The environments are unique to each of us because our lives are all unique. Moreover, if we are intended to return to human form, as is the case with a near-death experiencer, physical manifestations may be structured to convey certain messages for integration into human life. This is particularly true for the hellish environments some near-death experiencers report. They may represent lessons yet to be learned or emotional states to be resolved.

The more human deaths we have experienced, the faster we acclimate to the transition process, and the less likely we are, I believe, to manifest religious or Earthly scenarios or physical environments at all. I believe this is why during my own after death experience I was able to knowingly manifest Earthly scenery without being fooled by it, and why my experience included no religious features. I was familiar enough with the transition process to realize there is no true physicality to what is actually an entirely spiritual existence. And I was comfortable enough not to need physical manifestations.

Souls who are new to the transformation process, or whose human experience wears off more slowly, may be assisted by what humans call guides. Often we perceive these Light Being guides as Earthly loved ones who predeceased us, for they may assume the form of the loved ones' former and familiar human bodies or faces. Or they may take the appearance of angels, Jesus, or Buddha, if those forms would help them relate to the awakening Light Being. These loving Light Beings' jobs are to reassure and comfort the confused new arrival and smooth the transition in any way they can. Often they communicate telepathically, but in the human language of the abandoned host. They may explain some or all of the process, or, conversely, if the soul is not ready to permanently abandon human life, these guides will remind it that its time of transition has not yet come.

The first acclimation we must undertake after absorbing the Light is acknowledging and accepting that we are dead, as humans understand that term. This awareness may come easy or hard, depending upon our evolutionary level and/or the circumstances of our host's death. Traumatic deaths are sometimes more difficult to process than those planned in advance. Some of us who have not been able in human life to admit to our own eternal existence, believing human existence is all there is, may take longer to cross this first transformative "hurdle." Light Being souls who do not readily accept their continued existence after leaving the body permanently may find themselves in a state of consciousness devoted entirely to coming to terms with this baseline fact. NDEr Dannion Brinkley has described it as, "a place where we dwell for as long as it takes to see ourselves as spiritual beings. It is the region of consciousness where we purge our personal misconceptions."[40]

Intermediate Stages. Various intermediate stages of the awakening process are triggered once we accept that we are "dead" to human life and have begun a spiritual transition process. We can now begin flexing spiritual "muscles." This is when a life review might take place, for that event requires completion of the initial stages of awakening so we can use the Light Being talent for multi-dimensional awareness. Other processes may include working through unresolved human emotions like fear and grief, bursts of "knowing" that educate us about our participation in an awakening process, or spiritual rest. Once we are acclimated to the new states of awareness and how they work, we may be ready to mentally reintegrate with that part of our Light Being that was not invested into the human life.

Full Awakening. As the amnesia of our human role wears off, that part of our Energy invested into the human body as soul rejoins the level of awareness of the full Energy field of our Light Being. We are complete! Whole again.

We can now recall our eternal memories. At first, the memories may just be from our own hundreds of lifetimes on Earth and elsewhere. Soon all of Universal Knowledge floods back to us. We know for certain that we are Light Beings, not human beings. We feel completely fulfilled and at peace. We acknowledge we are home. We understand fully that we are literally extensions of Source's awareness and consciousness, that we have never been separate from Source, and that human life was something like an illusion or role we played in a dream. We understand that as Light Beings in our natural state, not confined as we once were to human flesh, we have a wealth of abilities unknown to humankind.

We are telepathic. We move freely in all directions and have expanded senses. We have total recall of every detail of physical lives lived, including all the sensory data collected. Previously unremembered information comes to us instantly through a process called "knowing"; we do not have to study to learn. We can access Universal Knowledge on any topic of interest just by focusing our attention and intention on having that knowledge. I experienced all of these wonders. So will you.

We are able in our natural state to share our consciousness intimately with other Beings of Light through merger with them, thereby residing in a simultaneous joy of individuality and collective being. Merger into my five Light Being friends was one of the most otherworldly aspects of my own beyond-death experience. (See Chapter 21.)

Rejoining Light Being "Society". We may remain in our natural form and spend time in any number of Light Being "societies," or levels of awareness, between "lives" in physical form. Some who have journeyed where I have, and come back to human life to tell about it, might call these states of being actual places, levels of heaven, or other dimensions. Although I did not experience what I call Light Being society this time, my understanding from recapturing all my memories of life between lives in physical matter is that these levels or dimensions more closely resemble developmental stages of awareness than actual places. Human developmental stages include being an infant, a toddler, a youngster, a teenager, a young adult, middle-aged, and finally "old." Light Beings have similar developmental stages as they evolve back to the highest energy vibration and merger with the Source. For example, one developmental stage might be continuous study of human life experiences in an effort to understand how unconditional love might have been brought into the picture to change the outcome of a relationship event. Other Light Beings, at other developmental levels, serve their colleagues as guides to welcome new souls to the transformation, or as members of a soul's council of guidance, or as teachers or other helpers.

Merger into Source. Eventually, all of us, as well as all of creation, reintegrate back into Source and end the illusion of separateness forever. Some may be destined to rejoin the Source temporarily between what we would call "lives." My understanding from my own experience is that I was poised to dissolve back into Source, though I do not recall now whether it would have been forever or for a while.

Summary. I believe the reason why near-death experience stories vary so much, from just being out of body, to going into the Light, to meeting beings of some type, is because different experiencers go through different stages of the process of transforming back into a Being of Light. Most simply rise out of their bodies and observe its resuscitation, with a few traveling on the Earthly plane to visit friends or loved ones. Many see or even go into the Light. Those who experience later stages of the transformation may meet guides or Beings of Light who converse telepathically with them. A few, like me, go even farther and complete the transformation back to Light Being before being pulled back into the body. And a very rare few achieve knowing that they are but a point of awareness of Source, and, thus are ready to rejoin Source as part of its Collective Being of Light and Love. I understand that we all follow the same general process of transformation and would eventually have followed the same course I did, with the number and timing of stages and ultimate end point depending upon level of evolution and unique needs.

One of the many wondrous aspects of my experience was that it lifted me entirely out of the human perspective on both death and religion, and allowed me to participate in multiple simultaneous levels of perspective on the topic of what happens after we die. Though the available levels or frameworks of perception are innumerable, for ease of reference I have chosen some major demarcations in perspective within which to discuss the transition process we call death and entry into the afterlife. The following grid compares how I perceived each "stage" of the process as I passed through it, with how I later understood it from the vantage point of being connected to Universal Knowledge and then integrated into Source.

Level of Perspective

Step in Process	Human mode of thinking	Soul out of the body after death	From Light Being level of perspective	From Source's perspective
Getting out of body	Feels like dying.	Feels like being released from confinement.	Starts the shift to higher levels of awareness.	You were never truly in a body.

Step in Process	Human mode of thinking	Soul out of the body after death	From Light Being level of perspective	From Source's perspective
Traveling out of body	Ghosts. Discarnate lost souls.	Feels like out of body travel.	Represents lack of desire to abandon human mode.	Still feeling effects of human mode.
Entering black void	Creates fear that there is no afterlife.	Feels like being in a living cave.	Severs the tie to human form.	Temporary perception.
Going into the Light	Represents going to Heaven.	Feels like love is diffusing through spiritual body.	Represents first awareness of a shift in vibration.	Raising vibration enough to be aware of the One.
Seeing deceased loved ones	Resurrection of the body.	Guides to the afterlife.	Light Beings serving you to make the transition more comfortable.	Temporary perception.
Experiencing multiple levels of perspective	No concept.	Feels like exciting new talent.	Natural ability of Light Beings.	Innate ability as part of Source.
Manifesting reality	Heaven as Earthly pleasures.	Manifested physical environments feel as real as anything on Earth.	Manifesting Earthly scenes occurs before transition into Light Being.	Innate ability as part of Source.
Life review	Represents "the judgment."	Feels like everything you have ever experienced plus all the reactions of everyone else.	Opportunity to see whether you have met the goals you set before entering human life.	Purpose of life is to bring these experiences to the Source.
Beings of Light	Angels or religious figures.	Angels or religious figures or recognition that souls are Light Beings.	Light Beings showing themselves without human disguise.	A higher level of awareness than human.

226

Step in Process	Human mode of thinking	Soul out of the body after death	From Light Being level of perspective	From Source's perspective
Transforming into Being of Light	No concept.	Feels like waking up from a coma.	Natural end result of death process.	Transitioning to a higher vibration.
Remembering eternal life	No concept.	Feels like becoming whole again.	Integration of soul Energy into rest of Light Being.	Innate ability as part of Source.
Access Universal Knowledge	Channeling, psychics or mediums.	Feels like "knowing" is deposited directly into mind.	Natural state as Light Being.	Innate ability as part of Source.
Merger into other Light Beings	No concept.	Feels like total sharing of another's life.	Natural ability of Light Beings.	Represents higher integration into the One.
Merger into Source	No concept.	Feels like finally being home.	Ultimate end point of evolution.	Ultimate dissolution of illusion of self and reintegration into the One.

My experience opened my eyes to the knowledge that we are truly wondrous creatures, body and soul, and that nothing in our universe is as black and white as humans like to believe. Dying is no exception. It is a marvelous part of the cycle of life for the human being, who is born knowing that its lifespan is temporary, as well as a blessed release from temporary confinement for the eternal Light Being soul within.

20

Nanci's Death

My death began with the search for alien life—cancer cells.

A routine screening mammogram at age 43 revealed a suspicious pattern of calcium deposits, a telltale sign that raised enough questions to warrant an invasive breast biopsy. On the day of surgery, a radiologist performed a needle localization procedure where a large-bore needle with a wire inside was inserted into the calcifications. The needle was withdrawn and the wire left in place as a marker for the surgeon to cut around. Mammograms were used to center the needle among three lesions.

After the procedure, the doctor and radiology technician left to get the last set of films developed and, I suspect, take a much-deserved break. I stayed behind in a chair, trying to calm myself and slow my racing heartbeat. My last mundane thought was wondering whether I was going to be able to close my hospital gown over the wire sticking out of my chest.

A few minutes after the doctor and technician left I started to feel "funny" and feared I would black out. My efforts to get up and call for help were stymied by an overwhelming weakness. But instead of passing out, my body engaged in a slow process I can only describe as "essence withdrawal."

I become aware that "I" was slowly *pulling out* of the head, neck, and upper limbs of my body and compressing into an inner core about chest high. The weight and mass of my own flesh pressed in on me as I evacuated downward. The being I always thought of as "me" distilled out of its fleshy casing and quickly "whooshed" completely out of the body. I had a moment's distinct impression of being separated from, and standing completely intact in front of, my own sitting body. My sense was that "I" was whole; yet wholly out of my body.

Suddenly I flitted into a womb-like palpable blackness. Before I could fully adjust to it, I noticed light barely perceptible at the void's trailing edge. I remember thinking to myself upon seeing the light, "Oh, yeah, I know what this is. I'm supposed to go into the Light." Going into the Light seemed the natural thing to do, a habit even, but I did not mentally connect it to death because it was obvious *I was not dead!*

Upon entering the Light, a cocoon of energizing love enfolded me. The Light's effect on me was visceral, but somehow more than that. I was not just seeing and feeling the Light; I was literally becoming *part of* it. My concept of being a discrete life form began to dissolve, welcoming the Light and its love to diffuse through me.

Relief that my consciousness remained intact overcame me. I had survived whatever happened to me. My personality, memories, and thought processes were all still with me. I was MYSELF, whether in the body or not. *That body was not* ME as I had always assumed! Realization of who I really am flooded my mind.

While basking in that loving Light I rediscovered the truth: what we call the *soul* is my personhood, not the body. And I am a complete being, in and of myself, separate from that body. What survived death was actually the identity and personality I had always attributed to the human being. In short, I had it backwards. But not entirely backwards. For my body was not just a shell I had inhabited, or "the temple of the holy spirit" as I was taught. Now that it was gone, I could tell that the body had its *own separate personality*, emotions, thoughts and beliefs, which were now conspicuously absent.

I had previously assumed all my character traits to be human, reactions of the body I inhabited to the events of its unique lifetime. That belief allowed me to blame a lot of my faults on my parents. In the Light, however, I clearly saw that while this human lifetime did contribute much to my current memories, emotional maturity, and experiential knowledge, those parts of me were not solely human, and did not die with the body. They continued in my eternal personality. I finally understood the real ME. The true ME. The whole ME.

Early life in the Light was a series of discoveries in awareness and changes in perspective. I was not in a place so much as a frame of mind or state of being. It was all so wonderfully exciting! Yet part of my mind kept trying to diagnose my condition. I knew I had not blacked out because I was fully conscious—more conscious than I had ever been. Nevertheless, the nagging need to understand compelled me to inventory my sensations and emotions, looking for clues to a diagnosis.

I noted that while my essence glowed, and was clearly diffused outward like light, it had a core concentrated into some type of being with a vague form I did not see. Otherwise, I could see wherever I thought to look–front, back and sides—360 degrees. But there was nothing to see but Light. Everything else physical, of course, was gone. No heartbeat. No breath sounds. No feeling of heat or cold. No physical sensations at all.

All pain was gone. Interestingly, I missed it. I had been used to feeling an undercurrent of constant pain from weight lifting and a neck injury. I had no skin to itch or burn. No joints to ache. No cuts or bruises to groan when touched. These sensations all seemed to last far too long when experienced on Earth. But there, in the Light, the pain of a lifetime was but a moment's poignant remembrance. Now that pain was gone, the true impact of the magnificence of being "in the body" hit me full force. My body's pain was an eloquent expression of life—human life! It reminded me that I enjoyed the ultimate privilege of having a material body that could interact with matter and feel things a spirit cannot.

Though pain had vanished, I still had emotions, all of which had been heightened to a degree impossible in human form. The intense love I first thought was coming *from* the Light now radiated through and from *me*. Immense love, joy, and bliss filled me. My emotions were projecting into the Light and being returned to me, magnified tenfold, in echoes or ripples. It was the most incredible, wonderful feeling of being high on happiness.

Overlying the bliss, like a canopy, was wonder, and curiosity of a magnitude I had never experienced in human life, though learning had been one of my greatest pleasures.

I could feel surprise, for much of what happened to me was breathtakingly surprising. Like the fact that I missed the feeling of being alive in a way only a human body can feel. No more could I snuggle into another person's loving embrace, or feel soft breezes on my face, rain pelting my head, or sunshine roasting my skin. These and many other sensations humans take for granted were now lost to me. I no longer felt the comfort of heat or crispness of cold, the swish of clothing, the rise and fall of my chest as I breathed in and out, my own heartbeat, hunger, thirst, or physical desire. There was nothing to taste in the Light. And I missed the taste of chocolate. I felt these losses as a wistful release, like a sigh.

Suddenly it hit me. I understood. How foolish I had been for taking these human gifts for granted. How arrogant and spoiled rotten! So many precious moments of physical pleasure ignored as though my body and soul were deadened to them. So much attention to what *might* happen, or had happened, and so little to the glory of the now. So much focus on working instead of living. The body had been a wonderful treasure trove of sensory input, but I chose most often to block it out in pursuit of the allegedly higher purpose of becoming a success.

Though my inventory of sensations disclosed that all my other emotions continued, one all too familiar one was gone—fear. I felt no fear whatsoever, even from clearly being in unfamiliar territory. While in the body I would have found the inability to control my surroundings uncomfortable. More than that, I would have been extremely anxious over not knowing what would happen next. I never realized before how much fear had controlled my human life. Many, many of what I had considered normal, logical viewpoints were revealed to me as mere masks of fear. Fear of disapproval. Fear I would be judged unworthy of love and respect. Most of all, fear of being wrong. I did whatever it took to avoid situations where I might be proven wrong. Those fears all seemed so silly to me once I discovered fear is strictly a human condition. I was so grateful those fears were all gone, replaced by an unbelievable flood of love and sense of well being.

These thoughts reminded me of my body, which I saw was somewhere to the right and below where I was in the Light. I knew the body was not me, yet I was still surprised to discover I had no more emotional attachment to it than to the chair holding it. Observing the body fortified with this new detachment triggered an instant understanding of the duality of our human existence– human being infused with immortal soul. I knew the body to be a very loving and giving human animal that consented to blend with me so that I might take physical form. But the body is definitely a separate being from me. The body *died* March 14, 1994. I, on the other hand, became much more *alive*.

Siddhis

Wondrous new intellectual skills bombarded me as I adjusted to my new life. I intuited that these skills are native to us, no matter how foreign they seemed at my still semi-human functional level. They felt familiar, like rediscovered favorite old clothes, yet intensely exciting at the same time.

The human way of thinking began slipping away as I transitioned into an awareness of what I *recognized* as my "natural state." Thinking became effortless, extremely clear, and lightening fast. It felt like I finally had *full* use of my intellect versus what in comparison was sluggish half-wittedness experienced in the body.

Knowing. A vast hodge-podge of information unknown to me in human form spontaneously sprang to life in my mind as a collective whole called "knowing." Even the term for it, the word "knowing," popped into my mind unsolicited. "Knowing" is a sensation of understanding imbued with both the conviction of scientific validation and the richness of personal experience. In other words, the information feels as proven as the fact that the Earth is round, and as much first-hand knowledge as my own childhood. "Knowing" informed me that understanding gained through "knowing" is the truth—Universal Knowledge available to all who inhabit the Light.

The off-hand appearance of "knowing" that humans

completely misunderstand mental illness surprised me. After college graduation I had considered becoming a psychologist, returning to campus to secure a degree in psychology in furtherance of that plan. Understanding how humans treat tender souls whose unique gifts and advanced evolution earn them the label "crazy" saddened me greatly.

Many, many insights then crowded my mind as I embraced otherworldly delights. Those I recall grace the pages of this book.

Multiple Levels of Awareness. Life in the Light thrilled me with the ability to literally hold multiple simultaneous levels of perspective on my own self-awareness. There is nothing like it in human experience. I could hold a thought, observe myself intentionally generating that thought, be aware of myself as both thinker and observer, and marvel at my own multiple awareness levels—all instantaneously and simultaneously. There were many more awareness levels as well. Each layer or level felt like a complete consciousness unto itself. It seemed I could expand my perspective ever farther outward, while still seeing and feeling each previous level of consciousness like layers of a wedding cake.

The experience of multiple levels of awareness was layered over a simultaneous acknowledgement that I was transitioning into another type of life form. I knew intuitively from this experience that I had left human life far behind.

Manifesting Reality. As my spiritual awareness expanded, my contact with what I had always thought was reality contracted.

Reality literally became what I made of it.

Having seen my body some distance away made me wonder again where I was. I could not be dead, I reasoned. I never felt more alive, conscious, and awake. Besides, I had always heard that when you die you go through a tunnel to the Light at the end. I was already in the Light without going through a tunnel, so I could not be dead. While I was thinking this thought, a tunnel suddenly appeared! A classic concrete reinforced tunnel materialized before me as though it were a conduit through a mountain's imposing façade. This tunnel was just as solid and real to me as anything I had ever perceived while in the body. Its dank outer walls enclosed me as I moved and blocked my view of what lay beyond.

Since I had been in the Light for some time now, I knew this tunnel did not herald death. Clearly though, I reasoned, there had to have been some relationship between my thought "tunnel" and its magical appearance.

To find out, I intentionally thought to myself, "I've also heard it [the afterlife] described as a beautiful meadow or valley." Immediately a verdant meadow full of wildflowers nestled between purple-hazed mountains stretched out before me. It was just as real as the tunnel, and everything I had experienced while in the body, with one exception—when I was on Earth, my surroundings were there *before* I consciously thought about them. In this place, I knew I instantly created the meadow just by thinking the word. I knew it was not "real," despite its sense of "reality" as I had experienced reality while in the flesh.

This experiment confirmed my suspicion that in the Light all I had to do was think about an environment to create it in "reality." The term "manifesting" popped into my mind as the name for this phenomenon. *I could manifest reality.* I knew the tunnel and meadow appeared only because I thought about them. I personally manifested a tunnel and meadow into reality just by thinking the words. The manifestations were *so real* I did not trust my senses. So I conducted one more experiment to verify I actually produced those thought-forms myself.

My test thought was, "I have only passed out and dreamed the rest and am now awake and on my way over to surgery." Immediately I was walking along a hospital corridor. Yellowish tiled institutional walls ran parallel beside me. My feet felt solidly planted on uncarpeted floor. I heard hospital din above the swish of my body moving beneath the hospital "johnnie" as I sensed the closeness of the nurse escorting me to the Cancer Hospital. It was *soooo* very real. Yet I knew for certain I was in the Light, not the Hospital.

I *remembered* suddenly that in our natural spirit state we manifest anything and everything we want with instantaneous results. We literally manifest reality as we go. Though dumbstruck by how real and solid as matter those manifestations were, I realized they were different than solid matter on Earth, because I knew I had projected them as reality via my own thoughts. They did not fool me as they do while I am in the body. What? I thought with surprise. Fool me?

In response to this self-examination I *remembered* that I likewise manifested reality while imbedded in human form. I manifested my Earthly surroundings, just as I did in the Light, but I did so *unconsciously*. The essential ingredient is belief. I believed the Earth exists apart from my manifesting it because those around me believed it. I grew up believing in Earth life as it unfolded from the birth of Nanci's body. I understood then that we all manifest what we believe, and if those beliefs are passed on from human generation to generation, then the same manifestations persist.

The simple truth of our ability to manifest reality is Earth-shattering. It means I can change my surroundings, my life, through application of this spiritual power. And if I can do it, so can you. If we collectively and concertedly *consciously* use our ability to manifest we can literally change the world we live in. It is, after all, just a collective manifestation in the first place.

21

✳ Life As a Being of Light

Enlightenment and wonder wove through my life in the Light like meandering country roads on a map. On one track I knew I was in my "natural state" as a spirit. Intersecting that was the realization that being in a human body is a temporary state. Forty-three years of believing I was human drained out of me like dirty oil from a car as I continued my awakening.

Accepting my spiritual nature reoriented me to the need to focus my attention outward to get my bearings. Doing so, I noticed five more brilliant lights of different hues in the distance. The lights were spectacular, gorgeous glowing tints that conveyed depth, like gazing into pools of fathomless water. Soon familiarity registered; I knew names for these colors in words that sounded like an alien language. But no color I had ever experienced in human life compared to these distant Light beams. They were alive in a way that light cannot be on Earth.

The five bands of colored light confused me at first. I had not expected more than the one Light I entered at death's doorway. The colors seemed to have varying depths, as though some were farther away than others, like layers or levels stretching out before me. For a moment I wondered how to "follow the Light" like a beacon when there were five of them, when Beings suddenly appeared just to the left of and under the array of lights. It seemed Beings had come forward from within the colored lights to meet me.

The Beings were entirely luminescent, aglow from within, and brilliant as the sun, though their light affected my vision no more than the reflected light of the moon. Their Energy shone as different unearthly hues from core to periphery, signifying to me varying characteristics, like densities or temperatures. The Beings also had quite visible brilliant auras fanning out in halos of exquisite radiance. They appeared to occupy space, but all I could see of a body was a vague outline of a head and shoulders. I perceived no physical matter to them, just Energy and Light. I knew I had not manifested these beings, for they were quite unlike anything I had ever imagined. My mind called them Beings of Light, for they seemed more like pure energy than anything of a traditional religious nature like angels (though I can certainly see why others might call them angels).

To my delight I was not surprised to see these Beings, nor they to see me. I soon recognized them as my most beloved, dearest, warmest, wonderful friends/family/soul mates—my eternal loved ones. Not one of them was anyone I had ever known on Earth. Yet I knew these glorious Beings of Light instinctively. I also understood the instant I recognized them that I too am a Light

Being, that what I had been calling my "self" is actually a Being of Light. I was finally HOME!

I recalled my dear friends' one-word names in a language that would be foreign sounding on Earth, but was deeply known to me there. I *knew* these Light Beings intimately, and well. Instead of how separate from me other humans feel, these friends seemed more like *part of me* as well as distinct beings in their own right.

I felt completely at ease with these Light Beings, as well as expected, welcomed, enfolded, completely accepted, and loved in the unconditional sense. My heart could not grasp how loving and accepting these Beings were. They were "my people" in what seemed like a race or species of beings. The sense of belonging was overpowering.

As a result of this reunion I fully *remembered* who I *really* am—a powerful, immortal Being of Light the same as my friends. I could not *believe* I had been so fooled into thinking I was a human being. All my human concepts of what it means to have a soul went out the window. Never before this experience had I even dreamed that what we call souls is an actual separate race of beings from humans. I could feel my friends were slightly amused by these realizations on my part, in an older, wiser kind of way, like a parent who watches a child find out on her own that mother really does know best.

So I decided to direct my concern about which colored light to follow to the five Beings. One or more of them *thought* back to me in English: "It doesn't matter. Just pick one and follow it." Implicit in that simple instruction was the unspoken fact that they were all leading me to the same place.

The Beings then telepathically conveyed emotions to me I would translate into language to be, how was it? Or, how'd it go? Did you do it? What did you see and hear and feel? Show us everything. My impression was that everyone but me understood that I had been sent on a journey into human life in an effort akin to an assignment or mission, and my friends wanted a full report. The sensation was like coming out of a coma and realizing everyone around you knows what happened to you but you, and they have been eagerly awaiting your regaining consciousness.

These Light Beings were not destined to be guides in the traditional role described by others who have crossed over. My impression was they loved me so much they could wait no longer, and so had rushed ahead of the "rest of us" like rambunctious children. That was the English phrase that came to me—the "rest of us"—though everything else was conveyed telepathically. Somehow I knew I would shortly be joining "the rest of us." I sensed I was being processed through pre-determined stages of transition from the human experience to my natural state as a Being of Light. And my best friends were too excited about my return to wait any longer to share my life.

In our natural state we do not have the impediments of either amnesia or linear time. So an entire lifetime on Earth is remembered all at once, in vivid detail. I lovingly shared these memories with my soul mates. I could feel they were eager and excited to not only hear, but to literally *experience,* my life on Earth. Soon I understood that by telepathically sharing my life memories with them, my friends could actually *live my life and experience it* in much the same way I had. By this I mean they could share in my life either as an onlooker or as a participant, as they chose. They could watch Nanci's life like a movie on a screen in their minds, or live within my memories as a participant in the events as they transpired. And this would all happen simply by expanding their awareness to include my just-ended life.

Although I had heard that your whole life passes before your eyes when you die, I had no real idea what that meant until actually experiencing it. My life as Nanci flashed before my spiritual eyes as one integrated whole while my friends enjoyed it. It did not unfold like a movie, or progress in sequence. The whole lifetime was just there, all of it, in minute detail in current memory, and playing out all around me as if on a soap bubble. Imagine standing inside a soap bubble watching light refract all around its surface. You would see pink, and purple, and pearly hues of all descriptions—the colors translucent, swirling and blending as they glide across the bubble's surface. What I saw was similar, though instead of colors, events from my life as Nanci floated over the bubble's surface, out of sequence and bleeding into each other. All the sights, sounds, smells of a lifetime surrounded me. I was reliving it all again. All at once. Yet I was also outside events, as if inside the center of the bubble, watching it impartially. Both experiences transpired simultaneously.

One of the Light Beings entered inside my life with me, *living* my life as Nanci with me, experiencing all the emotions and physical sensations I had while living it. Another one seemed to be on the filmy outer edge of the bubble, blinking in and out of scenes sampling my life's events, living the roles of various other people. The other three were standing outside the bubble, just watching my life. My Light Being friends were able to participate in events from any "time" in my life because all events existed simultaneously for them. I was able to witness them doing this because my consciousness had somehow blended into theirs.

Not only was everything I had ever said, done, and thought there on the bubble of my life review, but also every sensory input from the body—everything I saw, heard, and felt. All the data I had gathered as a human form was right there for reliving. For example, I remember having a panoramic view of all the skies I have ever observed: the gray, cloudy Ohio skies outside my office window; "severe clear" blue skies seen from my airplane cockpit; sunny ocean vacation skies; stormy, lightening-filled heavens of West Virginia springs.

My Light Being friends were absolutely thrilled with it all, even all the events I thought were horrible, or that had caused me great pain, suffering, or agony. They found it all truly wonderful. And they were watching it, living it, feeling it, and emoting in ways humans would lamely interpret as, "wow, this is great stuff."

As I felt their reactions, I was amazed the Light Beings were not judging me. They were not judging my life. They had no criticism for the horrible things I had done. Nor were they finding my life petty or unimportant. They just loved it—all of it. Unconditionally. I saw, through them, that life is all a matter of perspective and that the perspective I had while I was human was not necessarily the right one, or the only one. I realized with relief that I was not going to be judged in this afterlife. The Light Beings were not judging me and I intuited no one higher up would, either. The loving Beings were actually proud of me for enduring my human life, for having had the experiences, and for just having been brave enough to take physical form. I do not mean "proud" in the human sense here. My friends did not care whether I made one choice or another, only that I had the courage to accept the challenge of human life. My gratitude for their loving compassion would have made me weep, had I eyes to do so.

The only one judging me during the life review was *me*, and I was doing it from a regained perspective of unconditional love. As I re-experienced my just ended human life, I felt very keenly how badly I had sometimes made other people on Earth feel, how selfish and unloving I had acted on occasion, though I was totally unaware of it at the time. Actually living others' emotional reactions to me was as real as the manifestations I created earlier. All their emotions were true, and in present time. Literally participating in the consequences of my own choices from the various perspectives of others affected by my behavior impacted me far more than could a simple pronouncement of displeasure by any God. Knowing that my Light Being friends could see every mistake I ever made, and every unloving thing I ever did, shamed me more than their displeasure could have, for I believed I was repaying their unconditional love with unworthy experiences.

I saw vividly that my so-called human accomplishments meant absolutely nothing. My lifelong pursuit of money, security, reputation, and material goods seemed so embarrassingly infantile in comparison to what I now knew to be the reality of my existence as a pure Light Being. Seeing my forty-three years of hard work reduced to a moment's flash before my eyes made my human life feel unimportant. The fact that my successes contributed nothing to my goal of achieving unconditional love disappointed me greatly. Not even the twenty-one full-time years of education, or the sporadic legal, art, and assorted other classes for sixteen years after that, carried any weight in my own life review court. The only part of my life's efforts that mattered was what I had learned about how to treat other people. And I had not learned nearly enough.

Simultaneously—another multiple layers of awareness experience—while reliving every minute detail of my just-ended life on Earth, I reawakened to eons of my own personal memories, experiences, emotions, and everything that makes me a unique

Being. The clearest explanation might be to say that the part of my Energy that had been my human body's soul was reunified with the rest of my full Light Being Energy. It was similar to a simultaneous computer upload and download occurring within my own mind.

As engrossing as the life review was, all my interest in it evaporated as soon as I realized all of my memories were back. But more than just memories returned. I was aware of layer upon layer of additional consciousness I can only describe as "the rest of me," or "my memories and knowledge of who I really am," or "my full database," or "recovering from amnesia." As it was happening, I knew for certain that what I was accessing were my own personal memories of my lives (in human terminology) before and after I came to Earth as Nanci.

I was flabbergasted by the memories of hundreds or thousands of "lifetimes" returning to me, for in all the years I had thought I understood what the Church meant when it said our souls are immortal, I do not recall ever being told that it means I existed *before* birth into this particular human life. I assumed immortality started after death from this current human life. But here they were—my memories of earlier corporeal lives and eons of life as a Being of Light—as proof I existed prior to Nanci's human life.

The terms "remembered" and "memories" are especially apt in this context. It was not at all the sensation of learning something new. I *recognized my own* memories, thoughts, and knowledge. Things I had forgotten while in human form. Remembering as a Being of

Light has no comparison to remembering while in human form. Human remembering takes a little effort. The details are fuzzy and slow to come to mind. Parts of an event are not recalled at all. As a pure Light Being, the sensation was instant total recall with crystal clarity.

There was also a qualitative difference to the remembering; it came to me in the form of "knowing" and "understanding." By this I mean information was not communicated in words, symbols, or even pictures. It was deposited "whole" into my awareness with a sense of total physical and mental understanding in context. I not only remembered the information, but I felt it, and knew it experientially. It parallels the difference between reading a book about being a cowboy and actually riding a horse and herding cattle under an open sky. The knowledge was all first-hand.

As the memories flooded back I was thunderstruck by how I could possibly have forgotten it all! I was *amazed* by the degree of amnesia I experienced in the flesh. My eternal life had been an unending series of lifetimes as humans and other species, interspersed with periods of time lived in contemplation among the Light Beings. Over and over again I had chosen parents for their ability to provide an offspring I could inhabit in order to experience the events and situations I needed for my own evolution. Human life was nothing more than a classroom to me, an incubator for personal growth.

The emotional impact hit me like a proverbial blow to the chest to experience "knowing" that my just passed life on Earth was not my *real life* at all. It was like a role in a play or dream, a mere portrayal of life in comparison to the fullness and reality of my true life in the Light. I felt as if I was just waking up from a very long sleep, or coming out of a coma. It was *unbelievable* to me how completely fooled I had been into thinking there was nothing more to life than my human existence. It was patently absurd to me that I could have believed my human life was reality at all.

Excitement at witnessing the breadth and variety of the lives I had chosen was surpassed only by the shock of the truth that it was all *my choice!* Every bit of it. No one else planned any life for me. And, though I did have help early in my evolution choosing physical hosts, my own desire for growth and learning in particular areas is mostly what drove my choices. Beyond that, I understood that I have played out every conceivable aspect of different relationships, and have chosen particular lives just to experience different viewpoints and perspectives on the same relationship. There are so many perspectives! All my life as Nanci I had thought my own perspective was the "right" one, the most well informed, the most objective and fair. What a laugh. There are more perspectives than stars in the sky!

As my soul mates and I drifted through the colored rays together, my consciousness transformed in a way that cannot be described in human terms. The best I can do is approximate. The other Light Beings and I expanded our awareness outward to encompass each other's thoughts. Doing so, I realized I had always had unlimited access to all their knowledge, as well as the Knowledge of the Universe. It just took a little effort to flex my awareness muscles enough to include more than I was used to in human form.

"Knowing" came to me that I was undergoing the normal process of melting off the human veneer and fully awakening to my natural state. The deluge of information flooding my mind was not new to me. Rather, the human amnesia that kept me from remembering it had been stripped away. Trying to explain it from the human perspective makes it seem like the information was coming from outside; yet it was not. Some words that attempt to convey the sensation might be "epiphany," "revelation," "awakening," or "enlightenment," but these terms are feeble in comparison to the actual experience.

Zillions of gigabytes of information roared through my mind like floodwaters through a canyon, and, amazingly, I absorbed and understood it all! All the Knowledge of the Universe temporarily exploded into my mind. Answers to all my questions about who we are, why we are here, and who God is, were right there in my mind (see Part I). Finally I understood what life is all about. It is so very simple! In fact, the truth is so divinely simple I failed to see why we are not just given this information outright.

In response to my righteous anger over having had this information hidden from me while on Earth, a panorama of the entire history of religion among humans played out in my mind like a documentary. (This will be related in a future book.) As the future of planet Earth unfolded before my mind's eye, I witnessed its evolution unconcerned, convinced I would not be returning. Consequently, I made no great effort to remember the future until I realized that I was once again going to be commingled with the human body. Even then, I succeeded in clutching only these few glimpses of future (post-2007) events as I spiraled back into physical matter:

* Habitation on Earth spans three time and life cycles identified to me as "epochs," each lasting thousands and thousands of years. We are currently near the end of the Second Epoch. My best recollection is that it will terminate around 2013-2015 when a more pronounced transition to the Third Epoch will begin. I cannot be certain of the exact date because such details did not survive my re-entry into the body, despite my best efforts to retain them. But my sense is that the current Epoch ends during my remaining human lifetime, which I estimate to end around 2033.

* The transition to the Third Epoch will not be as abrupt or devastating as that heralding the Second Epoch. Entire species, including humans, will not be extinguished, although the human population will be decimated by natural disasters and disease. But I saw no global war

destroying mankind. No nuclear wars at all.

* Hundreds of disasters played out on my mind's viewing screen, starting after the turn of the millennium and becoming more frequent and more intense as the Second Epoch comes to a close. Included were earthquakes, tidal waves (tsunamis), floods along the coastlines and riverbeds, freakish weather changes, glacial melts, volcanic eruptions, and the spread of new epidemics of old bacteria and viruses that had mutated. I recognized one such disaster in 2002, an earthquake in Japan, looking at pictures in the newspaper. The 2005 tsunami is another example. Many more will follow. The mutations of cold viruses into SARS and avian flu viruses into deadly strains are consistent with what I saw of the transition's diseases.

* I saw the United States in relief-map format with parts of the East Coast missing or flooded, including New York City and bedroom communities up and down the East Coast sunk below water level; Florida's peninsula was missing; the Mississippi River overflowed such that Louisiana was under water, along with half of each state to the immediate north; and the West Coast was missing from just south of Big Sur to Mexico. Mountains formed the coastline of Southern California, but I do not recall which mountain range.

* A global view disclosed that Japan was gone. Simply gone. I do not recall the responsible cataclysm.

* I saw the collapse of the world's financial system. A fellow near-death experiencer, Ned Dougherty, writes in his book *Fast Lane to Heaven*, that, "The financial and banking institutions will collapse due in large part to the failure of the insurance companies as a result of the natural disasters. The United States will be thrown into political, economic, and social chaos."[41] This prediction sounded accurate to me when I read it and would explain what I saw during my review of Earth's future.

* The upcoming transition to the Third Epoch does not constitute the "End of Days," as that term is used in Christianity. A third and final epoch of peace and spiritual evolution on Earth follows the transition from the Second Epoch. The human population is greatly reduced, inasmuch as only those evolved enough to participate in this tranquil era survived the transition. Those who did survive appear to be of two types: those with sufficiently mutated DNA to be called a new human species, and those who accelerated their own personal growth and raised their vibration.

My sense, as of this writing, is that when and how the transition between epochs proceeds will depend in large part upon humankind's actions during the next decade. Our collective conduct, particularly how we handle natural disasters and whether we stop our global destruction of the environment, will affect the extent of the physical devastation and creation of new deadly viruses. For example, continued pollution will hasten climatic changes. Continued "development" of jungle and rain forest lands is very likely to release into the population new viral infections for which we have no cure.

The degree of stress and suffering each individual will experience during the transition will depend upon his/her vibration and evolutionary level. Both can be increased between now and then through application of the principles outlined in Part II. Increasing our individual and collective awareness of our Light Being nature will ease us into the Third Epoch with fewer individual and global disruptions. That evolution comes at a price, however. We must abandon old myths and beliefs and see the truths of the universe as they really are, rather than as humans would like them to be. The truths are inside us. Seek them there.

As the review of Earth's lifecycle ended, my attention refocused on the present moment, only to discover I had expanded my awareness so far outward as to join that of the other Light Beings— literally. My awareness/consciousness had *merged into* their Energy, their awareness/consciousness. We had become part of each other in the same way that molecules of air are part of the atmosphere and drops of water form the ocean. My earlier impression of a species of actual beings was dispelled when we all transformed into pure thought Energy without form.

I realized after this merger that I had access to all of my friends' memories, thoughts, and emotions. I could literally *experience* their existences, the same way they had experienced mine during my life review. It was possible in this state to actually feel like I was someone else entirely, like I was living and experiencing life as though I were one of my friends.

We were merged beings. Yet I retained my own identity, personality, thoughts, memories, and emotions. Both existences were possible simultaneously in this state. Just by shifting my attention I switched back and forth between the familiarity of the singular personality I knew as myself and living as a collective being of six. There is nothing remotely like it in human experience.

The six of us then experienced something akin to forward momentum as a collective entity seeking to rejoin "the rest of us"—those my friends had left behind to be the first to welcome me home. Instantly, I knew for certain that the Collective Being called "the rest of us" is Source. And as I inched closer and closer to Source's core, the faster I raced through levels of consciousness and perspective. I began to understand more and more of what was going on in the universe.

Being this close to Source invested me with the understanding that I do not exist as a separate being from Source. This newly gained insight, that I am merely a point of Source's own awareness or one of its thought-forms, burst the bubble of illusion of my individuality. No longer could I deceive myself into thinking I am "real," in the way humans use that word. I am but one tiny level of consciousness of a Being holding zillions and zillions of forms of consciousness. From the human perspective, I would be like a dream character. Not real. Someone Source thought up in order to experience what it would be like to be . . . well, me. The gloriousness of the realization that I am actually Source *thinking* exceeded my wildest imaginings about who I am and the ultimate disposition of my life. I am Source. We all are.

Hovering moments from total immersion into it, I absorbed a mind-blowing new understanding of our Supreme Being and how we fit into the grand scheme of things (as described in Part I). I learned that some of our commonly held beliefs about life and our relationship with our Creator are like photo negatives—where we see the inverse of the real picture. These reversed or backwards perceptions deprive us of so much joy and love that could be ours in this human life, if only we could see the developed full-color picture as I did. If more people understood the nature of our connection to each other and the Creator it would be impossible for us to treat each other with the hatred and indifference that predominate our society. Truly understanding how we came to be, and that we are ourselves literally part of the entity we call God, would grant us the peace and unconditional love we seek with all our hearts.

My five friends and I were about to merge completely back into Source. It was so humbling. So unspeakably . . . intimate. Moving. Overwhelming. There are no words. I deeply understood that I am Source, an integral part of Source. And Source so loved itself, and loved that little spark of itself that became me, that it allowed me to venture out and experience this illusion of having a separate identity—of being a separate person. Of having all these lives, and all these experiences, and all these wonders, and all these loves–just so that I would feel separate and special, fulfilled, and excited. And then Source brought me back into itself so I could remember that I have never been alone. That I have never been separate. That all of those times of feeling small, worthless, or powerless were just an illusion, so that I could come back into Source and appreciate how much love it feels for me. How much power I really have. How incredibly spectacular we really are. Because I never would have appreciated those things without the contrast of human life.

I understood that rejoining Source would give me access to the thoughts, emotions, and experiences of the zillions of its other points of awareness or thought-forms in the same way I had shared merged Energies with my five companions. And through merger I would know what Source does about its own existence and its source. Could there be a more wondrous heaven than this? I was so sublimely happy! Words cannot begin to express the overwhelming love, beauty, joy, and feeling of completeness I experienced. How I wished everyone could feel this way all the time!

I never accomplished complete merger back into the Source, however. Something pulled me backwards, out of immersion into my loved ones. I was spiraling back to my physical body. Initially I believed I never would have chosen not to rejoin Source. The separation was *horrible.* Yet it was familiar. I *did* choose it—as I had done many, many times before.

In my mind, there could be no greater testament to the unconditional love of our creating Source than the fact that it allowed me to make the ultimate choice: the choice to continue the illusion of being a separate identity. The choice to leave the most incredible bliss in favor of the challenges of human life. I was allowed to choose, as though my will was more important than Source's dominion over its own thoughts. It would have been so simple for Source to just "unthink" me as a character in its vast databank of life forms and return its thoughts to itself. The tenderness and acceptance with which Source treated my wish to return to human life astounded me—and still does.

22

Back Into the Body

Rejoining the body took perhaps seconds—but sufficient time to experience a transition back to human perspective, similar to, though shorter than, the one going from human to Being of Light.

A sensation of being sucked backwards by a great force tore at my willpower to stay with Source. Deep within my memory, I recognized the cyclonic effects of a return to the body. Through my disorientation I could actually feel layers of awareness stripping off my consciousness, like Band-Aids ripped off skin. Faster and faster I descended through awareness levels until I could no longer assimilate the changes. Memories of Universal Knowledge, and of my own eternal life, faded away as my desperate attempts to cling to them afforded all the tenacity of a sleeper clutching dreams.

My previously crystal clear thinking frayed at the edges and grayed out. Thoughts tumbled around and through each other, tattered debris in the funnel cloud of transition. Colors. Pictures. The only thought I could seize unyieldingly was the one invading my mind telepathically, "Love is what truly matters." It became my orienting mantra. "Love is all that matters." I vowed to spread this message back on Earth.

I slammed back into the body some time after the radiologist and technician returned to the mammography room and started reviewing the mammograms on the view boxes at the back of the room. I did not want to go into Nanci's body, but there appeared to be no other choice. I actually resisted going back. I resisted with all my might. I desperately wanted to keep all my memories and the Universal Knowledge I had regained. I mourned the loss of weightlessness, telepathy, instant total recall, and multiple levels of awareness.

The difficulty of getting back into body proved far greater than getting out of it. At first, "I" occupied only the body core, the same as I had before blasting out of it. It took real effort to force myself all the way back into my arms, neck and head, especially the brain and senses. The body felt heavy, wet, confining, restrictive in motion and senses, and dull of intellect. I imagine this is what it would feel like to be forced to put on an extremely tight, heavy wetsuit made out of clay. The sensation that I was sticking my limbs into monster flesh, flesh that is not really part of me, repulsed me.

Continued effort was required to push "me" all the way back into the arms, neck, and head. I felt like I was a compressed essence in the core of these structures and had to percolate out into all the cells. I could hear from *inside* my head, as though there were an inner spatial distance between my hearing and the body's ears. I could see from a point of reference behind the eyes, like looking through tubes at the outside world with the focus somewhere behind the retinas.

The radiology team had their backs to me, so I had to speak to get their attention. I whispered, "I passed out." The doctor and technician turned to look at me. The doctor seemed surprised to hear I had passed out and called a nurse right away. The RN brought a blood pressure cuff and pumped it up. I was vaguely aware of the doctor and nurse ministering to me while I worked to reclaim full use of the physical body. Every act required so much more effort than I remembered. I felt disconnected from skin and surface muscles.

The doctor asked if I knew who I was. I nodded yes. She then asked whether I knew where I was, and I opened the mouth to say, "Yes, in the mammo room." The radiologist asked if I knew who she was. After trying hard to think, I responded, "You look familiar, but I can't place you." That was the truth. She did seem familiar, but I could not recall why I was in a mammography room. Minutes later, I finally pieced together what must have happened. Eventually, I returned to normal as I dissolved back into the body. Nothing was said about my death, though the Hospital posted a nurse beside me for the rest of the day.

Weeks later, the official diagnosis I was given of my beyond-death experience was either a sudden severe drop in blood pressure (though I had no other symptoms of this condition), or an anaphylactic allergic reaction to the local anesthetic. The latter appears to be more likely, as I nearly died the second time I was given the same drugs.

The breast surgery was a huge success. After two weeks of nail-biting waiting, I learned no malignancy was found, though three "pre-cancerous" lesions had been removed. The body recovered completely and is now thirteen years post-op with no evidence whatsoever of any breast cancer.

Spiritually, I did not recover for many years.

Near-death researchers would characterize my beyond-death experience as "transcendental," meaning that it was longer and more complicated than most, and centered around the human condition and solutions to life's problems rather than anything strictly personal to my life. The personal aftereffect, however, was to emblazon upon my heart a guiding mission for the rest of this life: to tell as many people as I can what I remember of our true nature and purpose on Earth, and that "love is all that matters."

One of our purposes is our collective mission to speed up body/soul evolution closer to our Light Being nature, so that the transition to the Third Epoch will not hinge again on global destruction of the human species. It was very clear to me from my review of Earth's history and future that the collective intentions of everyone on Earth would determine when and how the Second Epoch would end—like the first one did, with the planet's human population destroyed, or with a less intense and slower transition to an enlightened era of peace and harmony.

In addition, each of us has an individual mission to understand our dual natures of Light Being soul inhabiting a human being, to become aware of our intrinsic grandeur as part of Source, and to restructure our daily lives to synchronize the vibrations between our bodies and souls by reducing the conflict between them through the application of unconditional love. Doing so will increase tenfold our happiness as Earth-bound adventurers.

Finally, it is time to know deep in our hearts that love is all that truly matters. Unconditional love is giving to others even when they do not know we have done it. Giving when it is impossible for others to appreciate it. Giving love unselfishly—to all, at all times. My gift of love was to return to this life, though I had no parents, husband, or children awaiting me. To return and continue to be a catalyst in other people's lives, to share what I now know to be true, and to witness the upcoming end of the epoch. To feel all alone in this world, knowing that home is just a stopped heartbeat away.

23

Conclusion

You must be willing to change your perspective to know who you really are. You are a powerful spiritual being with tremendous abilities that if used regularly would change your life and improve the whole planet. You are not limited to human perspectives, to human talents and skills. You have the right and responsibility to get to know your true self—what you are now calling the soul of the human body you inhabit.

Resolve to *live* your life. All of it, human *and* eternal.

Consciously live each second of every day. Choose the events of your life with eyes wide open to how they will impact your own spiritual growth, as well as the entire universe around you. We evolve through experiences and how we handle them. So you must present yourself with experiences in order to grow. Do not close yourself off to new experiences.

Do not spend your days chained to efforts to fulfill only basic survival needs. Spice your life with activities that trigger more of your Light Being nature. Use meditation to gain insight and Universal Knowledge, and reading to spark natural curiosity on any topic. Engage in creative endeavors of every type. You do not have to be a gifted artist or concert pianist. But do spend time creating—a story, a new recipe, a child's toy, a garden nook, or a gadget or tool—and allow that task to bubble creativity up within you.

Stop your preoccupation with the physical appearance of your host body. We deceive ourselves into believing that the one totally transient aspect of our existence, the human body, is the most important. Our culture constantly fosters identification solely with our bodies in both subtle and overt ways. Physical appearance is intensely important in American society and supports an immense advertising industry for every conceivable product. Gender determines career opportunities. Race poses hurdles to success, as though skin color dictates skill, judgment and intelligence. None of these physical attributes survives death of the body. Yet the *real* person, the personality of the Light Being inside the body, is overwhelmingly ignored in our society in favor of the physical packaging. *You* are being ignored. We have placed our emphasis on the wrong being. Our priorities are backwards.

Do not squander your time here chasing human measures of success that will die with your body. You will live on to regret that promotion or public recognition during your life review if you allowed human greed to lead you around by the nose. Working at a job or profession is not living. Work is one part of human life, a part that satisfies the animal survival instinct. And that is all it is. Your job does not define you. It does not make you who you are. Making your mark on history—of the world or of one company—

has no more eternal impact than taming tigers in your dreams. You will not care one little bit about that when you awaken into Light Being splendor.

No amount of Earthly business success, scientific achievement, or power over other human beings contributes in any way to the goal of learning how to live lovingly. We must treat each other with more love and respect if we truly want success in our lives—the kind of success that stays with us for all eternity.

Stop saying, "I had no choice," as an excuse for your behavior. You always have choice. And those choices always have consequences. Accept the consequences in a mature fashion, the same way you accepted the benefits of the choice when you made it. Honor each choice you make until you choose again, openly and legitimately. For example, if you have opted to be married, *be* married. Act supportive of your spouse. Be faithful to the vows you exchanged. Contribute half to the whole of family life. If you later find you can no longer live the life you have built, declare that condition to your spouse and work with him/her to separate your lives in a loving way.

Similarly, honor your parents for who they are to you. You selected your parents specifically because they could provide a life full of opportunities for you to learn and grow in the experiences you desired. You *chose* them. It was not an accident of birth. You wanted to join human lives with those of your parents. Respect that choice and resolve to live life in relationships with your parents. Do not abandon them. Or dishonor them. Their lives are just as hard as yours. They also left the bliss of living in the Light with Source so that you could accomplish your evolution. Their Light Beings are bound to yours in an eternal web of love so unselfish that they are willing to suffer the hardships of human life, as well as your insults and disrespect to them as you grow, just so you can evolve.

Your children chose you in the same way you chose your own parents. They are not little animals you created and with whom you can do anything you please. Human offspring are sentient beings in their own right, with very raw emotions. And they are infused with extremely self-aware Light Being souls since before birth. Those souls may even be more evolved, and wiser, than you as a parent. Yet each child chose you specifically to guide his/her human life on paths that would bring evolution of body and soul. Honor that choice, as well as your choice to have children. The impact a parent has on a soul affects it for hundreds of lifetimes. Take that role seriously, and live it with as much unconditional love as you can muster.

Every moment of life is precious. Sharing life with a human host is a gift of joy and sorrow, love and grief, wonders and boredom. More than that, human life is a great privilege. It is a privilege to have this glorious Earth as our home. A privilege to participate in the evolution of the human species while simultaneously evolving ourselves. Be grateful to the human race for allowing us to school ourselves emotionally at its knee. Be grateful to Source for creating you to have all the wonderful and horrible experiences you have witnessed and felt.

Most of all, do not be afraid. Fear is a human animal trait that can be overcome by allowing your true nature to infuse your daily life. No eternal harm can come to you, for you will automatically return to Source simply by virtue of the fact that Source is your origin. There is no other place for a Source thought-form to go. You cannot lose "heaven" no matter what you do. Yet choosing to live a life of service to others, of love toward all, will increase your happiness so much in this human life.

The truth about life and death is not a secret. It is just difficult to grasp with our human-bound ways of thinking. My death experience demonstrated that the road to "heaven" is a path of personal spiritual evolution—an evolution that comes from experiencing love and compassion for, and non-judging acceptance of, each other, as well as ourselves.

The purpose of this human life is how you relate to others— how you bring love into the world. Remember the mantra from my tumultuous return to the body, "Love is all that truly matters." Know in your heart that you are an eternal integral part of Source itself and live that basic truth. Infuse your life with as much unconditional love as possible. Practice it. Believe in it. Believe in the truth that your true nature *is* unconditional love, and let that nature shine through your thoughts, words and deeds, now and forever.

We are actually non-physical beings who have chosen to experience human lives—but in the process we have also chosen to abandon our spiritual powers. That is not necessary. And it is such a waste. We *can* be conscious of our true nature while in the body. We *can* use our natural spiritual talents while in human form to increase our love and happiness here. It does not have to be all or nothing for us, and it should not remain our decision to choose to use so little of our God-given talents.

NOTES

Preface

[1] Barbara R. Rommer, M.D., *Blessing in Disguise: Another Side of the Near-Death Experience*. (St. Paul: Llewellyn Publications 2000), citing, G. Gallup and W. Proctor's *Adventures in Immortality: A Look Beyond the Threshold of Death* (McGraw-Hill 1982). During 1980-81, this Gallup Poll surveyed a representative sample of the American population for answers to the following question, included within a much larger study of beliefs about life after death: "Have you, yourself, ever been on the verge of death or had a 'close call' which involved any unusual experience at that time?" Dr. Rommer's book was published six years after my own experience and, thus, had no influence on what I perceived in the Light.

[2] Raymond A. Moody, MD, *Life After Life* (New York: Bantam 1975). Dr. Moody's definition is an event that encompasses, among other elements, some of the following: leaving the body, witnessing resuscitation efforts and news of one's own death and accurately describing those events, hearing sounds or voices after leaving the body, feelings of peace and painlessness, going through darkness and a tunnel or vortex, seeing or going into a very bright Light, having a life review, being in another "world" or place, meeting Beings of Light, knowing things about the future, being told to return to human life, and returning to the body.

[3] Rommer, *Blessing in Disguise*, 3.

[4] The thriller *Flatliners*, starring Julia Roberts, Kevin Bacon and Keifer Sutherland, explored this topic when a group of medical school residents took turns flatlining on an EKG monitor and then resuscitating each other in order to see what type of near-death experience they would have.

[5] Sam Parnia, M.D., Ph.D., *What Happens When We Die* (Carlsbad, CA: Hay House 2006). Also, see generally, *The Journal of Near-Death Studies*, published by the International Association for Near-Death Studies, Inc., P.O. Box 502, East Windsor Hill, CT 06028.

Chapter 2

[6] During my beyond-death experience, I understood and accepted that the "God" of which we are part is only one of a race of such beings. This concept was so foreign to everything I had ever believed about the Universe, and so controversial for others to hear, that I rarely disclosed this relevation to others. I have discovered only one other writer who agrees: Neale Donald Walsch, in his

book *Conversations with God: An Uncommon Dialogue* (New York: G.P. Putnam's Sons 1996), Book 1, which was written two years after my beyond-death experience and could not have had any influence on my perceptions two years earlier. There God dictates to Mr. Walsch the following truth:

> Now I will tell you, there are even larger truths than this to which you will one day become privy. For even as you are the body of Me, I am the body of another.

You mean, You are *not* God?

> Yes, I am God, as you now understand Him. I am Goddess as you now comprehend Her. I am the Conceiver and the Creator of Everything you now know and experience, and you are My children . . . even as I am the child of another.

Are you trying to tell me that even God has a God?

> I am telling you that your perception of ultimate reality is more limited than you thought, and that Truth is more *un*limited than you can imagine.

Walsch, 197. All quotations from *Conversations with God* by Neale Donald Walsch, copyright © 1995 by Neale Donald Walsch used by permission of G.P. Putnam's Sons, a division of Penguin Group (USA), Inc.

7 Quoted from a message on the Near Death Experience Research Foundation Website, www.nderf.org, hosted by Jody Long, J.D., and Jeffrey Long, M.D., posted March 6, 2005, entitled "Richard L's NDE." Quoted with the permission of the Longs and Richard L.

8 P. Raymon Stewart, *Living as God: Healing the Separation* (Vancouver: Namaste Publishing 2005), 77.

9 Ibid., 31-32.

10 Walsch, 17-18.

11 Ibid., 23, 25.

Chapter 3

12 Dannion Brinkley with Paul Perry, *Saved by the Light: The True Story of a Man Who Died Twice and the Profound Revelations He Received* (New York: HarperCollins 1994). Although this book was published in 1994, it was not generally available until after my own death experience. I read it in December 1995 after watching the TV movie based on the book. Seeing this movie is what first alerted me to the fact that a near-death experience was a recognized medical phenomenon. It also assured me that I had not hallucinated the whole event.

13 Walsch, 25-26.

14 P.M.H. Atwater, *Future Memory* (Charlottsville: Hampton Roads 1999), 113.

Chapter 4

15 Walsch, 13-14.

16 Dannion and Kathryn Brinkley, *The Secrets of the Light: Spiritual Strategies to Empower Your Life . . . Here and in the Hereafter* (Las Vegas: Heart Light Productions 2004), x-xi.

17 Michael Newton, Ph.D., *Journey of Souls: Case Studies of Life Between Lives* (St. Paul: Llewellyn Publications 2001), 247-248. This book was printed seven years after my beyond-death experience and, thus, had no influence on my perceptions during that event.

Chapter 5

18 Rommer, xx-xxi.

19 Conversely, if you do not find a soul mate, it just means that was not your goal this life.

20 Rommer, 127. Ted Bundy was a famous serial killer who charmed his victims into trusting him.

21 Excerpted from the NDE account of Kacie, quoted in Rommer, 143.

Chapter 6

[22] Excerpted from the NDE account of Sadhana, quoted in Rommer, 137.

Chapter 7

[23] Walsch, 40.

Chapter 10

[24] Eckhart Tolle, *The Power of Now: A Guide to Spiritual Enlightenment*, (Novato, CA: New World Library/Namaste Publishing 1999), 14-15, quoted with permission of Namaste Publishing.

[25] Ibid., 16-17.

[26] Michael Brown, *The Presence Process: A Healing Journey into Present Moment Awareness* (New York: Namaste Publishing/Beauford Books 2005), 5, quoted with permission of Namaste Publishing.

[27] Ibid., 165.

[28] There are a number of books written about "Somatic Experiencing ®" or its equivalent. One of my favorites is *Focusing* by Eugene T. Gendlin, Ph.D., available from Bantam Books and amazon.com. This book, originally published in 1978, condenses and makes readable the results of years of research and experimentation by a group of psychotherapists at the University of Chicago and elsewhere. Another somatic experiencing book that greatly helped me recover from the physical trauma of an automobile accident is *Crash Course: A Self-Healing Guide To Auto Accident Trauma & Recovery* by Diane Poole Heller, Ph.D. and Laurence S. Heller, Ph.D. While this latter book does specifically relate to auto accident victims, its principles apply to any type of physical trauma. It is also available from amazon.com.

[29] Brown, 165.

Chapter 11

[30] One of the more startling revelations during my life as a Being of Light was that not all human beings are inhabited by Light Being souls. Some are simply not chosen. Others may have been abandoned as hosts once the souls inside completed their goals or missions. This "knowing" is consistent with the Universal Knowledge I received about humans constituting a separate race or

species of beings from Light Beings, as non-scientists would use those words, capable of living without us inside.

[31]   Deborah Tannen, Ph.D., *You Just Don't Understand: Women and Men in Conversation* (New York: Ballantine 1990), 25.

Chapter 12

[32]   On-line Journal of Christina Potter, May 14, 2005, quoted with her permission.

Chapter 14

[33] According to Deepak Chopra, M.D., and David Simon, M.D. in their lectures entitled *Training the Mind; Healing the Body*, available on CD from Nightingale-Conant Corp.

[34]   Candace B. Pert, Ph.D., *Molecules of Emotion: The Science Behind Mind-Body Medicine* (New York: Simon & Schuster 1999).

[35] Available from the Namaste Publishing website and amazon.com.

Chapter 17

[36] Brown, 143-144.

Chapter 19

[37] *Stedman's Medical Dictionary*, 25th ed., s.v. death.

[38] *Webster's New Collegiate Dictionary*, s.v. death.

[39] I believe this is what accounts for so many near-death experiences. The soul then returns to the body to complete its pre-arranged human lifetime.

[40] Brinkley, *The Secrets of the Light*, 48.

Chapter 21

[41] Ned Dougherty, *Fast Lane to Heaven: A Life-After-Death Journey* (Charlottsville: Hampton Roads 2001), 253.

BIBLIOGRAPHY

Atwater, P.M.H., *Future Memory*. Charlottsville: Hampton Roads, 1999.

Brinkley, Dannion, with Paul Perry, *Saved by the Light: The True Story of a Man Who Died Twice and the Profound Revelations He Received*. New York: HarperCollins, 1994.

_____, and Kathryn Brinkley, *The Secrets of the Light: Spiritual Strategies to Empower Your Life . . . Here and in the Hereafter*. Las Vegas: Heart Light Productions, 2004.

Brown, Michael, *The Presence Process: A Healing Journey into Present Moment Awareness*. New York: Beauford Books/Namaste Publishing, 2005.

Chopra, Deepak, M.D., and David Simon, M.D., *Training the Mind; Healing the Body*. Niles, IL: Nightingale-Conant, CD.

Dougherty, Ned, *Fast Lane to Heaven: A Life-After-Death Journey*. Charlottsville: Hampton Roads, 2001.

L., Richard, *Richard L's NDE*, Near-Death Experience Foundation, www.nderf.org.

Moody, Raymond, Jr., M.D., *Life After Life*. New York: Bantum Books, 1975.

Newton, Michael, Ph.D., *Journey of Souls: Case Studies of Life Between Lives*. St. Paul: Llewellyn Publications, 2001.

Parnia, Sam, M.D., Ph.D., *What Happens When We Die*. Carlsbad, CA: Hay House, 2006.

Pert, Candace B., Ph.D., *Molecules of Emotion: The Science Behind Mind-Body Medicine*. New York: Simon & Schuster, 1999.

Rommer, Barbara R., M.D., *Blessing in Disguise: Another Side of the Near-Death Experience.* St. Paul, MN: Llewellyn Publications, 2000.

Stewart, P. Raymond, *Living as God: Healing the Separation.* Vancouver: Namaste Publishing, 2005.

Tannen, Deborah, Ph.D., *You Just Don't Understand: Women and Men in Conversation.* New York: Ballantine, 1990.

Tolle, Eckhart, *The Power of Now: A Guide to Spiritual Enlightenment.* Novato, CA: New World Library/Namaste Publishing, 1999.

Walsch, Neale Donald, *Conversations with God: An Uncommon Dialogue, Book 1.* New York: G.P. Putnam's Sons, 1996.

Index

ABOUT THE AUTHOR

Nanci L. Danison holds a BS Magna Cum Laude in biology, with a concentration in anatomy and physiology, a BA Magna Cum Laude in psychology, and a Doctorate in Jurisprudence. Until 1994, she was living the life of a successful trial lawyer in a large midwestern law firm. She often lectured on a national level and wrote on legal topics for the health care industry. Nanci at one time appeared on the Noon News for local TV stations in public service spots for the Bar Association, one of the activities that earned her a Jaycees' Ten Outstanding Citizens Award for community service. Then she had a near-death experience (NDE).

After her NDE, Nanci left the security of her big law firm and started a successful solo practice in health law, where she continues to be recognized for her legal abilities. Nanci's activities post-NDE include starting a local chapter of the International Association for Near-Death Studies, Inc.; earning a pilot's license in 2000, and Private Investigator's license in 2001; and sharing her NDE memories publicly. Nanci still practices law and writes books on what she remembers from her experiences in the Light. Contact her at www.BackwardsBooks.com.

Also by Nanci Danison

<u>Tapes and CDs</u>: *Light Answers to Tough Questions Series* of tapes and CDs. Available for order at <u>www.BackwardsBooks.com</u>

<u>CD</u>: *Light Answers to Tough Questions: A Life Plan,* a presentation at the International Association for Near-Death Studies, Inc.'s 2005 National Conference, available at <u>www.iands.org</u>

QUICK ORDER FORM

Fax: Fax this form to AP Lee & Co. at 614.798.1998
E-mail: <u>APLeeCo@sbcglobal.net</u>
Mail: AP Lee & Co., PO Box 340292, Columbus, OH 43234

Please send me *Backwards: Returning to Our Source for Answers* in:
☐ hardcover book form $23.95 _____ copies
☐ softcover book form $19.95 _____ copies
☐ CD $14.95 _____ copies

Please send me *Backwards Workbook* in:
☐ softcover book form $14.95 _____ copies

Consult <u>www.BackwardsBooks.com</u> for information on ordering CDs and tapes from Ms. Danison's *Light Answers to Tough Questions* series of workshops.

Please send free information on: ❏ future books
❏ presentations and workshops
❏ how to schedule Ms. Danison to speak to a group

Name: _____

Address: _____

City: _____ State: _____ Zip: _____

Telephone (if we have questions): _____
     E-mail: _____